WOMEN'S LIBERATION
IN THE
TWENTIETH CENTURY

PROBLEMS IN AMERICAN HISTORY

EDITOR

LOREN BARITZ
State University of New York, Albany

WOMEN'S LIBERATION
IN THE
TWENTIETH CENTURY

EDITED BY

Mary C. Lynn

Skidmore College

John Wiley & Sons, Inc.
New York • London • Sydney • Toronto

Library of Congress Cataloging in Publication Data:
Main entry under title:
Women's liberation in the twentieth century.

  (Problems in American history)
  CONTENTS: Critiques of woman's role: Goldman,
E. Marriage and love. Gilman, C. P. The lady of
the house. Gilman, C. P. Socializing the house-
hold industries. Sanger, M. Birth control. East-
man, C. The status of women.—Unsolved problems:
Catt, C. C. Wanted; a new department. Martin, A.
Feminists and future political action. Seabury, F.
G. Stereotypes. [etc.]
    1. Feminism—United States—Addresses, essays,
lectures. 2. United States—Social conditions—
Addresses, essays, lectures. I. Lynn, Mary C.,
1943-

HQ1426.W664   301.41′2′0973   75-9570
ISBN 0-471-55738-2
ISBN 0-471-55742-0 pbk.

Printed in the United States of America

10 9 8 7 6 5 4 3 2 1

SERIES PREFACE

This series is an introduction to the most important problems in the writing and study of American history. Some of these problems have been the subject of debate and argument for a long time, although others only recently have been recognized as controversial. However, in every case, the student will find a vital topic, an understanding of which will deepen his knowledge of social change in America.

The scholars who introduce and edit the books in this series are teaching historians who have written history in the same general area as their individual books. Many of them are leading scholars in their fields, and all have done important work in the collective search for better historical understanding.

Because of the talent and the specialized knowledge of the individual editors, a rigid editorial format has not been imposed on them. For example, some of the editors believe that primary source material is necessary to their subjects. Some believe that their material should be arranged to show conflicting interpretations. Others have decided to use the selected materials as evidence for their own interpretations. The individual editors have been given the freedom to handle their books in the way that their own experience and knowledge indicate is best. The overall result is a series built up from the individual decisions of working scholars in the various fields, rather than one that conforms to a uniform editorial decision.

A common goal (rather than a shared technique) is the bridge of this series. There is always the desire to bring the reader as close to these problems as possible. One result of this objective is an emphasis on the nature and consequences of problems and events, with a deemphasis of the more purely historiographical issues. The goal is to involve the student in the reality of crisis, the inevitability of ambiguity, and the excitement of finding a way through the historical maze.

Above all, this series is designed to show students how experienced historians read and reason. Although health is not contagious, intellectual engagement may be. If we show students

something significant in a phrase or a passage that they otherwise
may have missed, we will have accomplished part of our objective. When students see something that passed us by, then the
process will have been made whole. This active and mutual
involvement of editor and reader with a significant human problem will rescue the study of history from the smell and feel of
dust.

Loren Baritz

PREFACE

The readings gathered in this volume have been selected to provide students with an opportunity to analyze the ways in which Americans viewed the changing role of women in the twentieth century. I first became aware of the need for such a collection when teaching a unit on the women's liberation movement as part of an introductory American Civilization course. Although my students were aware of the suffragist movement, they had some difficulty in understanding the relationship between nineteenth century advocates of women's rights and contemporary feminism, and had very little information on the period between the adoption of the nineteenth amendment to the Constitution in 1920 and the resurgence of feminism in the 1960s. Furthermore, their perspective on the first wave of feminism was slanted, focusing only on the struggle for the vote and not including other reforms. This book is designed to fill those gaps, to provide not only new information, but to indicate some of the conflicting definitions of "women's role" so that students may arrive at their own definitions.

Many colleagues and friends have helped to prepare this book. I wish to thank Loren Baritz for inviting me to do this volume, and also for his helpful suggestions. I am most grateful to Wayne Anderson, editor at John Wiley & Sons, for his encouragement and his patience. Gloria Moore and Barbara Smith, reference librarians at Skidmore College, were especially helpful in arranging interlibrary loans and tracking down hard-to-find material. Special thanks go to my secretary, Selma Harwood, and to two of my students, Jane Feinberg and Sandy Gibson, who helped to prepare the manuscript. My husband David Clark has, with his affection and his companionship, made a contribution for which I am deeply grateful.

Mary C. Lynn

Skidmore College
January 1975

CONTENTS

WOMEN'S LIBERATION
IN THE
TWENTIETH CENTURY

Introduction

Until quite recently, historians have ignored most questions concerning the position of women in this country, with the possible exception of the woman suffrage movement. Authors of standard American history textbooks who have included material on feminism have generally assumed that the problem of finding the appropriate economic, political, and social position for women was solved by the passage of the nineteenth amendment to the Constitution in 1920, giving women the vote, and apparently opening the door to full equality. In the best democratic tradition, according to this view, women were eventually liberated by being admitted to political power, and thus given the opportunity to remove any unfair restrictions that persisted. The social freedom exercised by some women during the 1920s is sometimes used to indicate the extent to which women achieved social liberation.

The development of a vociferous and highly visible women's liberation movement during the 1960s has challenged all these comfortable assumptions. Feminists have exposed the many areas where women have not achieved full equality with men, and a number of serious and careful efforts have been made to examine the roots of sex prejudice. Feminists no longer call for a single reform to accomplish women's liberation; they demand a host of changes, ranging from an end to discrimination in employment and salaries to public support for day-care centers, and reform of the educational system to eliminate sex-role stereotyping.

Whatever the outcome of this second feminist movement, its

1

existence has reawakened interest in the first wave of feminism, and in the progress of women between the apparent success of the suffragists in 1920 and the resurgence of feminism in the sixties. It is now even more important than ever to develop an understanding of the first feminist movement, including a consciousness of the critiques of woman's role that were made at the turn of the century, and an appreciation of what went wrong after 1920, when the suffragists prematurely celebrated their victory. Antifeminist theories, particularly from the period after the Second World War, when traditional domestic roles for women gained new popularity, must also be examined, as must the origins and development of the current women's liberation movement.

The readings collected in this volume have been assembled to facilitate such an examination of the ways in which the role of women in society has been defined. Feminists, antifeminists, and women's liberation writers are all represented here, because all show an intense concern for the "woman problem." By exploring the ways in which these men and women responded to the question of the role and position of women, we can gain new insight into the social history of this century, and new understanding of some of the problems we face today.

Feminism did not begin as an organized movement until some women had the leisure time to concern themselves with issues beyond mere physical survival. Although American feminists have been concerned with the problems of poor, black, and working-class women, feminism in this country has been in general a movement of white, middle-class women. This book reflects that bias: while black and poor women are certainly affected by the issues discussed here, the problems of class and race seem to have higher priority for those women. Thus the questions raised here, although they are relevant to all women, are raised by women of the middle class, for their middle-class sisters.

The movement for women's rights should not be studied in isolation, since its adherents have always expressed views reflecting the social and political currents of the day. In the years before World War I, feminist views could be expressed in a context of socialism or anarchism. Women's emancipation would be achieved, according to some advocates, as part of a general social upheaval that would change the whole structure of society. After the Bolshevik Revolution in Russia, and after the wartime persecution of socialists and anarchists, these views became less audible, as feminists articulated more conservative positions, urging women to work for reform within the system. Similarly, during the Eisenhower years, when social problems were generally ignored as middle-class Americans enjoyed increased affluence, women also turned inward and failed to see the problems inherent in the "feminine mystique." In the 1960s, as social action increased with the civil rights and antiwar movements, women again began to question their position and to work for increased emancipation. The radical ideas first expressed at the turn of the century gained new relevance during the 1960s, especially since little progress seemed to have been made in solving the problems that had suggested them.

The readings in this collection have been organized into five general areas to facilitate comparisons of the responses to similar problems of the different feminist generations, and to allow the student to place these ideas in historical context. Part One includes readings chosen to illuminate the various strands of feminist thought in the years before the passage of the nineteenth amendment. These selections should clarify the range of women's concerns, covering social, political, and economic issues. The readings in Part Two suggest some of the issues women faced in the two decades after 1920, including social reform, political activity, and very specific difficulties such as the need to eradicate sexual stereotypes and the problems of integrating marriage and a career. The evolution of what Betty Friedan has called "the feminine mystique" is considered in Part Three, which also includes a feminist critique of traditional thinking. Part Four contains writings from the current women's liberation movement, while Part Five consists of three different visions of what the future holds for women.

Whatever the future holds, women will consciously participate in the creation of new roles and life patterns. If we understand where we have been, perhaps we can better determine where we are going. There is considerable evidence that changes have begun, and that the roots of sexual prejudice are being attacked. We can never be quite the same again.

PART ONE

Critiques of Woman's Role

" Although some American women protested their social, economic, and legal restrictions in the eighteenth century, it was not
until the 1830s that women involved in the abolition movement
began to resist their limitations in an organized fashion. The
Seneca Falls convention in 1848, which issued a call to reform
based on the Declaration of Independence, was the first group of
women to demand the vote, although other women had worked
for legal and educational reforms prior to 1848. After the Civil
War, two national organizations, the American Woman Suffrage
Association and the National Woman Suffrage Association, were
formed to advance the progress of women. By 1890, when they
united as the National American Woman Suffrage Association,
both were firmly committed to the struggle for the vote. -

Although the tactics of the NAWSA were not particularly
militant, involving petitions, lobbying legislators, and calling for
referenda on the question of votes for women, the suffragists did
succeed in extending the franchise to women in four states by
1900. More importantly, suffragist activities encouraged women
to organize and to operate politically to achieve their goals. The
vote was seen as a primary step, leading to further gains in other
areas. The NAWSA, and the somewhat more militant Women's
Political Union, and Congressional Union, founded in 1907 and
1913, in response to the activities of militant British suffragists,
made no real attempt to question the role of women in the family, made no effort to examine marriage or motherhood, and
paid very little attention to the problems of employed women.

5

Indeed, feminist leaders had appealed to very conservative impulses in their effort to wrest one political concession from the men who held the power. Women, it was argued, would spread their benevolent maternal impulses over the nation, eradicating political corruption, balancing the votes of blacks and immigrants, and strengthening the political and social position of the educated middle class.

Yet there were feminists who rejected these positions, who failed to agree that enfranchisement was a supreme goal, who bravely attacked marriage, the family, and women's lack of access to birth control information as the chief agents of female oppression. It is much too simple to criticize the early feminists for their timidity in concentrating on a single issue—all feminists were not suffragists. And perhaps even the suffragists did not fully comprehend the complexity of the problem they faced: the way in which the prevalent myths regarding female nature combined religious, social, and economic values to limit women to a very restricted social role. A few feminists did understand these forces, and their critiques of woman's role sound surprisingly modern nearly 75 years later.

Emma Goldman (Reading 1) defined herself as an anarchist, while Charlotte Perkins Gilman (Reading 2) preferred to be called a socialist, but both, because of their intense desire to change the position of women in society, may be further defined as feminists. Both Goldman and Gilman examined the economic bases of woman's dependence, arguing that major changes in the structure of society had to occur before women could ever approach freedom. Because they were not particularly concerned to allay the fears of those holding power over the potential impact of admitting women to the electorate, they were able to make more objective analyses of woman's role than were their suffragist counterparts. Both were free to become theoreticians, and to develop a rational and internally consistent critique of American society. Even more important, both were able, in their own lives, to try to adhere to the political principles that they advocated. Although they did not agree on a solution to the problem they described, their definitions of that problem were quite similar.

Goldman and Gilman were not the only analysts of woman's role who were untempted by the simplicity of the suffrage argument. Margaret Sanger (Reading 3) is best known as a crusader for birth control, dedicated to making safe and effective contraception available to women of all classes. Sanger argued that the real liberation of women depended on reproductive freedom, on the right of women to control their own bodies. Sanger did not formulate the wide-ranging analysis of society as a whole that was characteristic of the writings of Goldman and Gilman, but she did come to grips with what was, at the time, an exceedingly delicate and sensitive issue. Her contraception clinics were raided by the police, and Sanger herself was jailed several times for violating obscenity statutes, but she continued in her efforts to provide birth control to women as a crucial step toward their eventual liberation.

Even women who were very much engaged in the struggle for the vote were capable of wider perceptions. Crystal Eastman, one of the founders of the militant Congressional Union for Woman Suffrage was well aware that many battles remained, once women had achieved the franchise (Reading 4). She saw that increased freedom would not automatically follow the passage of the suffrage amendment, but would have to be attained by continued organization, pressure, and struggle. Eastman is particularly noteworthy because she was a suffragist who was also very interested in economic and social problems, intimately concerned with the difficulties faced by working women, able to see some of the complexities of woman's role that went far beyond simple legal restrictions.

1 FROM   *Emma Goldman*

Marriage and Love

Emma Goldman (1869–1940), a Russian immigrant who came out of the sweatshops of Rochester to become an articulate and powerful advocate of anarchism, exemplified in her own life the principles she advocated in this essay. Although she could not identify with the middle-class organized feminists, Goldman was profoundly concerned with the question of women's liberation. Her critique of the position of women struck directly at the institution of marriage, which she condemned outright for restricting women, whatever their class, to lives of hypocrisy, passivity, and dependence.

The popular notion about marriage and love is that they are synonymous, that they spring from the same motives, and cover the same human needs. Like most popular notions this also rests not on actual facts, but on superstition.

Marriage and love have nothing in common; they are as far apart as the poles; are, in fact, antagonistic to each other. No

SOURCE: Emma Goldman, "Marriage and Love," *Anarchism and Other Essays*, Mother Earth Publishing Association, 1917. Reprinted by Dover Publications, 1969.

9

doubt some marriages have been the result of love. Not, however, because love could assert itself only in marriage; much rather is it because few people can completely outgrow a convention. There are to-day large numbers of men and women to whom marriage is naught but a farce, but who submit to it for the sake of public opinion. At any rate, while it is true that some marriages are based on love, and while it is equally true that in some cases love continues in married life, I maintain that it does so regardless of marriage, and not because of it.

On the other hand, it is utterly false that love results from marriage. On rare occasions one does hear of a miraculous case of a married couple falling in love after marriage, but on close examination, it will be found that it is a mere adjustment to the inevitable. Certainly the growing-used to each other is far from the spontaneity, the intensity, and beauty of love, without which the intimacy of marriage must prove degrading to both the woman and the man.

Marriage is primarily an economic arrangement, an insurance pact. It differs from the ordinary life insurance agreement only in that it is more binding, more exacting. Its returns are insignificantly small compared with the investments. In taking out an insurance policy one pays for it in dollars and cents, always at liberty to discontinue payments. If, however, woman's premium is a husband, she pays for it with her name, her privacy, her self-respect, her very life, "until death doth part." Moreover, the marriage insurance condemns her to life-long dependency, to parasitism, to complete uselessness, individual as well as social. Man, too, pays his toll, but as his sphere is wider, marriage does not limit him as much as woman. He feels his chains more in an economic sense. . . .

From infancy, almost, the average girl is told that marriage is her ultimate goal; therefore her training and education must be directed towards that end. Like the mute beast fattened for slaughter, she is prepared for that. Yet, strange to say, she is allowed to know much less about her function as wife and mother than the ordinary artisan of his trade. It is indecent and filthy for a respectable girl to know anything of the marital relation. Oh, for the inconsistency of respectability, that needs the marriage vow to turn something which is filthy into the purest and most sacred arrangement that none dare question or criticize. Yet that is exactly the attitude of the average upholder of marriage. The prospective wife and mother is kept in complete ignorance of her only asset in the competitive field—sex. Thus she enters into life-long relations with a man only to find herself shocked, repelled, outraged beyond measure by the most natural and healthy instinct, sex. It is safe to say that a large percentage of the unhappiness, misery, distress, and physical suffering of matrimony is due to the criminal ignorance in sex matters that is being extolled as a great virtue. Nor is it at all an exaggeration when I say that more than one home has been broken up because of this deplorable fact.

If, however, woman is free and big enough to learn the mystery of sex without the sanction of State or Church, she will stand condemned as utterly unfit to become the wife of a "good" man, his goodness consisting of an empty head and plenty of money. Can there be anything more outrageous than the idea that a healthy, grown woman, full of life and passion, must deny nature's demand, must subdue her most intense craving, undermine her health and break her spirit, must stunt her vision, abstain from the depth and glory of sex experience until a "good" man comes along to take her unto himself as a wife? That is precisely what marriage means. How can such an arrangement end except in failure? This is one, though not the least important, factor of marriage, which differentiates it from love. . . .

The moral lesson instilled in the girl is not whether the man has aroused her love, but rather is it, "How much?" The important and only God of practical American life: Can the man make a living? Can he support a wife? That is the only thing that justifies marriage. Gradually this saturates every thought of the girl; her dreams are not of moonlight and kisses, of laughter and tears; she dreams of shopping tours and bargain counters. This soul-poverty and sordidness are the elements inherent in the marriage institution. The State and the Church approve of no other ideal, simply because it is the one that necessitates the State and Church control of men and women.

Doubtless there are people who continue to consider love above dollars and cents. Particularly is this true of that class whom economic necessity has forced to become self-supporting. The tremendous change in woman's position, wrought by that mighty factor, is indeed phenomenal when we reflect that it is but a short time since she has entered the industrial arena. Six million women wage-earners; six million women, who have the equal right with men to be exploited, to be robbed, to go on strike; aye, to starve even. Anything more, my lord? Yes, six million wage-workers in every walk of life, from the highest brain work to the most difficult menial labor in the mines and on the railroad tracks; yes, even detectives and policemen. Surely the emancipation is complete.

Yet with all that, but a very small number of the vast army of women wage-workers look upon work as a permanent issue, in the same light as does man. No matter how decrepit the latter, he has been taught to be independent, self-supporting. Oh, I know that no one is really independent in our economic treadmill; still, the poorest specimen of a man hates to be a parasite; to be known as such, at any rate.

The woman considers her position as worker transitory, to be thrown aside for the first bidder. That is why it is infinitely harder to organize women than men. "Why should I join a union? I am going to get married, to have a home." Has she not been taught from infancy to look upon that as her ultimate calling? She learns soon enough that the home, though not so large a prison as the factory, has more solid doors and bars. It has a keeper so faithful that naught can escape him. The most tragic part, however, is that the home no longer frees her from wage-slavery; it only increases her task.

According to the latest statistics submitted before a Committee "on labor and wages, and congestion of population," ten per cent of the wage workers in New York City alone are married, yet they must continue to work at the most poorly paid labor in the world. Add to this horrible aspect the drudgery of housework, and what remains of the protection and glory of the home? As a matter of fact, even the middle-class girl in marriage can not speak of her home, since it is the man who creates her sphere. It is not important whether the husband is a brute or a darling. What I wish to prove is that marriage guarantees woman a home only by the grace of her husband. There she moves about in *his* home, year after year, until her aspect of life and human affairs

becomes as flat, narrow, and drab as her surroundings. Small
wonder if she becomes a nag, petty, quarrelsome, gossipy, unbear-
able, thus driving the man from the house. She could not go, if
she wanted to; there is no place to go. Besides, a short period of
married life, of complete surrender of all faculties, absolutely
incapacitates the average woman for the outside world. She becomes reckless in appearance, clumsy in her movements, dependent in her decisions, cowardly in her judgment, a weight and a
bore, which most men grow to hate and despise. Wonderfully
inspiring atmosphere for the bearing of life, is it not? . . .

As to the protection of the woman,—therein lies the curse of
marriage. Not that it really protects her, but the very idea is so
revolting, such an outrage and insult on life, so degrading to
human dignity, as to forever condemn this parasitic institution.

It is like that other paternal arrangement—capitalism. It robs
man of his birthright, stunts his growth, poisons his body, keeps
him in ignorance, in poverty and dependence, and then institutes
charities that thrive on the last vestige of man's self-respect.

The institution of marriage makes a parasite of woman, an
absolute dependent. It incapacitates her for life's struggle, anni-
hilates her social consciousness, paralyzes her imagination, and
then imposes its gracious protection, which is in reality a snare,
a travesty on human character. . . .

Love needs no protection; it is its own protection. So long as
love begets life no child is deserted, or hungry, or famished for
the want of affection. I know this to be true. I know women who
became mothers in freedom by the men they loved. Few children
in wedlock enjoy the care, the protection, the devotion free
motherhood is capable of bestowing.

The defenders of authority dread the advent of a free motherhood, lest it will rob them of their prey. Who would fight the
wars? Who would create wealth? Who would make the policeman, the jailer, if woman were to refuse the indiscriminate breeding of children? The race, the race! shouts the king, the president, the capitalist, the priest. The race must be preserved,
though woman be degraded to a mere machine,—and the marriage institution is our only safety valve against the pernicious
sex-awakening of woman. But in vain these frantic efforts to
maintain a state of bondage. In vain too, the edicts of the Church,

the mad attacks of rulers, in vain even the arm of the law. Woman no longer wants to be a party to the production of a race of sickly, feeble, decrepit, wretched human beings, who have neither the strength nor moral courage to throw off the yoke of poverty and slavery. Instead she desires fewer and better children, begotten and reared in love and through free choice; not by compulsion, as marriage imposes. Our pseudo-moralists have yet to learn the deep sense of responsibility toward the child, that love in freedom has awakened in the breast of woman. Rather would she forego forever the glory of motherhood than bring forth life in an atmosphere that breathes only destruction and death. And if she does become a mother, it is to give to the child the deepest and best her being can yield. To grow with the child is her motto; she knows that in that manner alone can she help build true manhood and womanhood. . . .

In our present pygmy state love is indeed a stranger to most people. Misunderstood and shunned, it rarely takes root; or if it does, it soon withers and dies. Its delicate fiber can not endure the stress and strain of the daily grind. Its soul is too complex to adjust itself to the slimy woof of our social fabric. It weeps and moans and suffers with those who have need of it, yet lack the capacity to rise to love's summit.

Some day, some day men and women will rise, they will reach the mountain peak, they will meet big and strong and free, ready to receive, to partake, and to bask in the golden rays of love. What fancy, what imagination, what poetic genius can foresee even approximately the potentialities of such a force in the life of men and women. If the world is ever to give birth to true companionship and oneness, not marriage, but love will be the parent.

2   FROM   *Charlotte Perkins Gilman*
The Lady of the House
and
Socializing the Household Industries

Charlotte Perkins Gilman (1860–1935) was the most important feminist theoretician the American movement produced. Although she identified herself as a socialist rather than a feminist, the bulk of her voluminous literary output was concerned with the woman problem. Strongly influenced by Thorstein Veblen, her work emphasized the waste of human and economic resources caused by the restriction of women to the domestic sphere. Gilman attacked the economic dependence of women in traditional marriage, dealing with sensitive issues that other women were reluctant to grasp. In these two selections, from The Home *(1901) and* Women and Economics *(1898), Gilman explores the pernicious effects on women of an institution most good Victorians held sacred, and proposes some alternative ways to meet human needs for food and shelter that do not necessitate the oppression of women.*

THE LADY OF THE HOUSE

The effect of the house upon women is as important as might be expected of one continuous environment upon any living creature. The house varies with the varying power and preference of the owner; but to a house of some sort the woman has been confined for a period as long as history. This confinement is not to be considered as an arbitrary imprisonment under per-

SOURCE: Charlotte Perkins Gilman, "The Lady of the House," *The Home,* (New York: McClure, Phillips, 1901). Reprinted 1972, University of Illinois Press.
Charlotte Perkins Gilman, "Socializing the Household Industries," *Women and Economics*, Small, Maynard & Co., 1898. Reprinted 1966, Harper Torchbooks.

15

sonal cruelty, but as a position demanded by public opinion, sanctioned by religion, and enforced by law. . . .

The animal mother is held by love, by "instinct" only; the human mother has been for endless centuries a possession of the father. In his pride and joy of possession, and in his fear lest some other man annex his treasure, he has boxed up his women as he did his jewels, and any attempt at personal freedom on their part he considered a revolt from marital allegiance.

The extreme of this feeling results in the harem-system, and the crippled ladies of China; wherein we find the women held to the house, not by their own maternal ties, of which we talk much but in which we place small confidence, but by absolute force. . . .

The extent and depth of this feeling is well shown by a mass of popular proverbs, often quoted in this connection, such as "A woman should leave her house three times—when she is christened, when she is married, and when she is buried" (even then she only leaves it to go to church), or again, "The woman, the cat, and the chimney should never leave the house." So absolute is this connection in our minds that numbers of current phrases express it, the Housewife—Hausfrau, and the one chosen to head this chapter—The Lady of the House.

Now what has this age-long combination done to the woman, to the mother and moulder of human character; what sort of lady is the product of the house? . . .

The house life, with its shade, its foul air, its overheated steaminess, its innumerable tiring small activities, and its lack of any of those fine full exercises which built the proportions of the Greeks, has not benefited the body of the lady thereof; and in injuring her has injured all mankind, her children.

How of her mind? How has the mental growth of the race been affected by the housing of women? Apply the question to men. . . .

The growth of the world has followed the widening lives of men, outside the home. The specialised trade, with its modification of character; the surplus production and every widening range of trade and commerce; the steadily increasing power of distribution, and transportation, with its increased area, ease, and speed; the ensuing increase in travel now so general and continuous; and following that the increase in our knowledge and love of one another; all—all that makes for civilisation, for progress, for the growth of humanity up and on toward the race ideal—takes place outside the home. This is what has been denied to the lady of the house—merely all human life!

Some human life she must needs partake of by the law of heredity, sharing in the growth of the race through the father; and some she has also shared through contact with the man in such time as he was with her in the house, to such a degree as he was willing and able to share his experience. Also her condition has been steadily ameliorated, as he, growing ever broader and wiser by his human relationships, brought wisdom and justice and larger love into his family relationship. But the gain came from without, and filtered down to the woman in most niggardly fashion.

Literature was a great world-art for centuries and centuries before women were allowed to read—to say nothing of write! It is not long since the opinion was held that, if women were allowed to write, they would but write love letters! In our last century, in civilised Christian England, Harriet Martineau and Jane Austen covered their writing with their sewing when visitors came in; writing was "unwomanly!"

The very greatest of our human gains we have been the slowest to share with woman: education and democracy.

We have allowed them religion in a sense—as we have allowed them medicine—to take; not to give! They might have a priest as they might have a doctor, but on no account be one! Religion was for man to preach—and woman to practise.

In some churches, very recently, we are at last permitting women to hold equal place with men in what they deem to be the special service of God, but it is not yet common. Her extra-domestic education has been won within a lifetime; and there are still extant many to speak and write against it, even in the Universities—those men of Mezozoic minds! And her place as active participant in democratic government is still denied by an immense majority, on the ground—the same old underlying ground—that it would take her from the house! Here, clear and strong, stands out that ancient theory, that the very existence of womanhood depends on staying in the house. . . .

The limitations of the house as an area for a human life are most baldly dreary and crippling in the lower grades, the great majority of cases, where the housewife toils, not yet become the lady of the house. Here you see grinding work, and endless grey monotony. Here are premature age, wasting disease, and early death. If a series of photographs could be made of the working housewives in our country districts, with some personal account of the "poor health" which is the main topic of their infrequent talk; we should get a vivid idea of the condition of this grade of house-bound life.

The lady is in a different class, and open to a different danger. She is not worn out by overwork, but weakened by idleness. She is not starved and stunted by the hopeless lack of expression, but is, on the contrary, distorted by a senseless profusion of expression. There is pathos even to tears in the perforated cardboard flytraps dangling from the gaudy hanging lamp in the farmhouse parlour; the little weazened, withered blossom of beauty thrust forth from the smothered life below. There is no pathos, rather a repulsive horror, in the mass of freakish ornament on walls, floors, chairs, and tables, on specially contrived articles of furniture, on her own body and the helpless bodies of her little ones, which marks the unhealthy riot of expression of the overfed and underworked lady of the house. . . .

In our immediate time the progress of industry has cut the lady off from even her embroidery. Man, alert and inventive, follows her few remaining industries relentlessly, and grabs them from her, away from the house, into the mill and shop where they belong. But she, with ever idler hands, must stay behind. He will furnish her with everything her heart can wish—but she must stay right where she is and swallow it.

> *Lady Love! Lady Love! wilt thou be mine?*
> *Thou shalt neither wash dishes, nor yet feed the swine!*
> *But sit on a cushion and sew a gold seam*
> *And feed upon strawberries, sugar, and cream!*

This amiable programme, so exquisitely ludicrous, when offered to the world's most inherently industrious worker, becomes as exquisitely cruel when applied. The physical energies of the mother—an enormous fund—denied natural expression in bodily

exertion, work morbidly in manifold disease. The social energies, boundless, resistless, with which she is brought more in contact every year, denied natural expression in world-service, work morbidly inside the painfully inadequate limits of the house. . . .
A modern "captain of industry" has a brain so socially developed as to require for its proper area of expression an enormous range of social service. He gets it. He develops great systems of transportation, elaborate processes of manufacture, complex legislation or financial manœuvres. Without reference to his purpose, to the money he may acquire, or the relative good or evil of his methods, the point to be noted is that he is exercising his full personal capacity.

His sister, his wife, has a similar possibility of brain activity, and practically no provision for its exercise. So great is the growth, so tremendous the pressure of live brains against dead conditions, that in our current life of to-day we find more and more women pouring wildly out into any and every form of combination and action, good, bad, and indifferent. The church sewing circle, fair, and donation party no longer satisfy her. The reception, dinner, ball, and musicale no longer satisfy her. Even the splendid freedom of physical exercise no longer satisfies her. More and more the necessity for full and legitimate social activity makes itself felt; and more and more she is coming out of the house to take her rightful place in the world.

Not easily is this accomplished, not cheaply and safely. She is breaking loose from the hardest shell that ever held immortal seed. She is held from within by every hardened layer of untouched instinct which has accumulated through the centuries; and she is opposed from without by such mountain ranges of prejudice as would be insurmountable if prejudice were made of anything real.

The obsequious terror of a child, cowed by the nurse's bugaboo, is more reasonable than our docile acquiescence in the bonds of prejudice. It is pleasantly funny, knowing the real freerom so easily possible, to see a strong, full-grown woman solemnly state that she cannot pass the wall of cloudy grandeur with Mrs. Grundy for gate-keeper, that seems to hem her in so solidly. First one and then another reaches out a courageous hand against this towering barricade, touches it, shakes it, finds it not fact at all, but merely feeling—and passes calmly through. There is really nothing to prevent the woman of to-day from coming out of her old shell; and there is much to injure her, if she stays in.

The widespread nervous disorders among our leisure-class women are mainly traceable to this unchanging mould, which presses ever more cruelly upon the growing life. Health and happiness depend on smooth fulfilment of function, and the functional ability of a modern woman can by no means be exercised in this ancient coop.

The effect of the lady of the house upon her husband is worth special study. He thinks he likes that kind of woman, he stoutly refuses to consider any other kind; and yet his very general discontent in her society has been the theme of all observers for all time. In our time it has reached such prominence as to be commented upon even in that first brief halcyon period, the "honeymoon." *Punch* had a piteous cartoon of a new-married pair, sitting bored and weary on the beach, during their wedding journey. "Don't you wish some friend would come along?" said she. "Yes," he answered—"or even an enemy!"

Men have accepted the insufficiencies and disagreeablenesses of "female society" as being due to "the disabilities of sex." They are not, being really due to the disability of the house-bound. Love may lead a man to "marry his housekeeper," and we condemn the misalliance; but he makes a housekeeper of his wife without criticism. The misalliance is still there.

A man, a healthy, well-placed man, has his position in the world and in the home, and finds happiness in both. He loves his wife, she meets his requirements as a husband, and he expects nothing more of her. His other requirements he meets in other ways. That she cannot give him this, that, and the other form of companionship, exercise, gratification, is no ground of blame; the world outside does that. So the man goes smoothly on, and when the woman is uncertain, capricious, exacting, he lays it to her being a woman, and lets it go at that.

But she, for all field of exertion, has but this house; for all kinds of companionship, this husband. He stands between her and the world, he has elected to represent it to her, to be "all the world" to her. Now, no man that ever lived, no series or combination of husbands that widowhood or polyandry ever achieved can be equivalent to the world. The man needs the wife and has her—needs the world and has it. The woman needs the husband—and has him; needs the world—and there is the husband instead. He stands between her and the world, with the best of intentions, doubtless; but a poor substitute for full human life.

"What else should she want?" he inquires in genuine amazement. "I love her, I am kind to her, I provide a good home for her—she has her children and she has me—what else should she want?"

What else does he want? He has her—the home and the children—does that suffice him? He wants also the human world to move freely in, to act fully in, to live widely in, *and so does she*.

And because she cannot have it, because he stands there in its stead, she demands of him the satisfaction of all these thwarted human instincts. She does not know what ails her. She thinks he does not love her enough; that if he only loved her enough, stayed with her enough, she would be satisfied. No man can sit down and love a woman eighteen hours a day, not actively. He does love her, all the time, in a perfectly reasonable way, but he has something else to do.

He loves her for good and all; it is in the bank, to draw on for the rest of life, a steady, unfailing supply; but she wants to see it and hear it and feel it all the time, like the miser of old who "made a bath of his gold and rolled in it.". . .

If the woman was fully developed on the human side she would cease to be overdeveloped on the feminine side. If she had her fair share of world-life she would expect of her husband that he be a satisfactory man, but not that he be a satisfactory world, which is quite beyond him. Cannot men see how deeply benefited they would be by this change, this growth of woman? She would still be a woman, beautiful, faithful, loving; but she would not be so greedy, either for money or for love.

The lady of the house may be most softly beautiful, she may be utterly devoted, she may be unutterably appealing; but all

her centuries of cherished existence have but brought us to
Punch's "Advice to Those About to Marry": "Don't!"....

*   *   *

WOMEN AND ECONOMICS

... Is it not time that the way to a man's heart through his
stomach should be relinquished for some higher avenue? The
stomach should be left to its natural uses, not made a thorough-
fare for stranger passions and purposes; and the heart should be
approached through higher channels. We need a new picture of
our overworked blind god,—fat, greasy, pampered with sweet-
meats by the poor worshippers long forced to pay their devotion
through such degraded means.

No, the human race is not well nourished by making the process of feeding it a sex-function. The selection and preparation of
food should be in the hands of trained experts. And woman
should stand beside man as the comrade of his soul, not the
servant of his body.

This will require large changes in our method of living. To
feed the world by expert service, bringing to that great function
the skill and experience of the trained specialist, the power of
science, and the beauty of art, is impossible in the sexuo-economic
relation. While we treat cooking as a sex-function common to all
women and eating as a family function not otherwise rightly
accomplished, we can develop no farther. We are spending much
earnest study and hard labor to-day on the problem of teaching
and training women in the art of cooking, both the wife and the
servant; for, with our usual habit of considering voluntary individual conduct as the cause of conditions, we seek to modify conditions by changing individual conduct.

What we must recognize is that, while the conditions remain,
the conduct cannot be altered. Any trade or profession, the development of which depended upon the labor of isolated individuals, assisted only by hired servants more ignorant than
themselves, would remain at a similarly low level.

So far as health can be promoted by public means, we are steadily improving by sanitary regulations and medical inspection, by professionally prepared "health foods" and by the literature of hygiene, by special legislation as to contagious diseases and dangerous trades; but the health that lies in the hands of the housewife is not reached by these measures. The nine-tenths of our women who do their own work cannot be turned into proficient purchasers and cooks any more than nine-tenths of our men could be turned into proficient tailors with no better training or opportunity than would be furnished by clothing their own families. The alternative remaining to the women who comprise the other tenth is that peculiar survival of earlier labor methods known as "domestic service."

As a method of feeding humanity, hired domestic service is inferior even to the service of the wife and mother, and brings to the art of cooking an even lower degree of training and a narrower experience. The majority of domestic servants are young girls who leave this form of service for marriage as soon as they are able; and we thus intrust the physical health of human beings, so far as cooking affects it, to the hands of untrained, immature women, of the lowest social grade, who are actuated by no higher impulse than that of pecuniary necessity. The love of the wife and mother stimulates at least her desire to feed her family well. The servant has no such motive. The only cases in which domestic cooking reaches anything like proficiency are those in which the wife and mother is "a natural-born cook," and regales her family with the products of genius, or those in which the households of the rich are able to command the service of professionals.

There was a time when kings and lords retained their private poets to praise and entertain them; but the poet is not truly great until he sings for the world. So the art of cooking can never be lifted to its true place as a human need and a social function by private service. Such an arrangement of our lives and of our houses as will allow cooking to become a profession is the only way in which to free this great art from its present limitations. It should be a reputable, well-paid profession, wherein those women or those men who were adapted to this form of labor could become cooks, as they would become composers or carpenters. Natural distinctions would be developed between the mere craftsman and the artist; and we should have large, new avenues of lucrative and honorable industry, and a new basis for human health and happiness.

This does not involve what is known as "co-operation." Co-operation, in the usual sense, is the union of families for the better performance of their supposed functions. The process fails because the principle is wrong. Cooking and cleaning are not family functions. We do not have a family mouth, a family stomach, a family face to be washed. Individuals require to be fed and cleaned from birth to death, quite irrespective of their family relations. The orphan, the bachelor, the childless widower, have as much need of these nutritive and excretive processes as any patriarchal parent. Eating is an individual function. Cooking is a social function. Neither is in the faintest degree a family function. That we have found it convenient in early stages of civilization to do our cooking at home proves no more than the allied fact that we have also found it convenient in such stages to do our weaving and spinning at home, our soap and candle making, our butchering and pickling, our baking and washing.

As society develops, its functions specialize; and the reason why this great race-function of cooking has been so retarded in its natural growth is that the economic dependence of women has kept them back from their share in human progress. When women stand free as economic agents, they will lift and free their arrested functions, to the much better fulfilment of their duties as wives and mothers and to the vast improvement in health and happiness of the human race.

Co-operation is not what is required for this, but trained professional service and such arrangement of our methods of living as shall allow us to benefit by such service. When numbers of people patronize the same tailor or baker or confectioner, they do not co-operate. Neither would they co-operate in patronizing the same cook. The change must come from the side of the cook, not from the side of the family. It must come through natural functional development in society, and it is so coming. Woman, recognizing that her duty as feeder and cleaner is a' social duty, not a sexual one, must face the requirements of the situation, and prepare herself to meet them. A hundred years ago this could not have been done. Now it is being done, because the time is ripe for it.

If there should be built and opened in any of our large cities to-day a commodious and well-served apartment house for professional women with families, it would be filled at once. The apartments would be without kitchens; but there would be a kitchen belonging to the house from which meals could be served to the families in their rooms or in a common dining-room, as preferred. It would be a home where the cleaning was done by efficient workers, not hired separately by the families, but engaged by the manager of the establishment; and a roof-garden, day nursery, and kindergarten, under well-trained professional nurses and teachers, would insure proper care of the children. The demand for such provision is increasing daily, and must soon be met, not by a boarding-house or a lodging-house, a hotel, a restaurant, or any makeshift patching together of these; but by a permanent provision for the needs of women and children, of family privacy with collective advantage. This must be offered on a business basis to prove a substantial business success; and it will so prove, for it is a growing social need.

There are hundreds of thousands of women in New York City alone who are wage-earners, and who also have families; and the number increases. This is true not only among the poor and unskilled, but more and more among business women, professional women, scientific, artistic, literary women. Our school-teachers, who form a numerous class, are not entirely without relatives. To board does not satisfy the needs of a human soul. These women want homes, but they do not want the clumsy tangle of rudimentary industries that are supposed to accompany the home. The strain under which such women labor is no longer necessary. The privacy of the home could be as well maintained in such a building as described as in any house in a block, any room, flat, or apartment, under present methods. The food would be better, and would cost less; and this would be true of the service and of all common necessities.

In suburban homes this purpose could be accomplished much better by a grouping of adjacent houses, each distinct and having its own yard, but all kitchenless, and connected by covered ways with the eating-house. No detailed prophecy can be made of the precise forms which would ultimately prove most useful and pleasant; but the growing social need is for the specializing of the industries practised in the home and for the proper mechanical provision for them.

The cleaning required in each house would be much reduced by the removal of the two chief elements of household dirt,—grease and ashes.

Meals could of course be served in the house as long as desired; but, when people become accustomed to pure, clean homes, where no steaming industry is carried on, they will gradually prefer to go to their food instead of having it brought to them. It is a perfectly natural process, and a healthful one, to go to one's food. And, after all, the changes between living in one room, and so having the cooking most absolutely convenient; going as far as the limits of a large house permit, to one's own dining-room; and going a little further to a dining-room not in one's own house, but near by,—these differ but in degree. Families could go to eat together, just as they can go to bathe together or to listen to music together; but, if it fell out that different individuals presumed to develop an appetite at different hours, they could meet it without interfering with other people's comfort or sacrificing their own. Any housewife knows the difficulty of always getting a family together at meals. Why try? Then arises sentiment, and asserts that family affection, family unity, the very existence of the family, depend on their being together at meals. A family unity which is only bound together with a table-cloth is of questionable value.

There are several professions involved in our clumsy method of housekeeping. A good cook is not necessarily a good manager, nor a good manager an accurate and thorough cleaner, nor a good cleaner a wise purchaser. Under the free development of these branches a woman could choose her position, train for it, and become a most valuable functionary in her special branch, all the while living in her own home; that is, she would live in it as a man lives in his home, spending certain hours of the day at work and others at home.

This division of the labor of housekeeping would require the service of fewer women for fewer hours a day. Where now twenty women in twenty homes work all the time, and insufficiently accomplish their varied duties, the same work in the hands of specialists could be done in less time by fewer people; and the others would be left free to do other work for which they were better fitted, thus increasing the productive power of the world. Attempts at co-operation so far have endeavored to lessen the existing labors of women without recognizing their need for other occupation, and this is one reason for their repeated failure.

It seems almost unnecessary to suggest that women as economic producers will naturally choose those professions which are compatible with motherhood, and there are many professions much more in harmony with that function than the household service. Motherhood is not a remote contingency, but the common duty and the common glory of womanhood. If women did choose professions unsuitable to maternity, Nature would quietly extinguish them by her unvarying process. Those mothers who persisted in being acrobats, horse-breakers, or sailors before the mast, would probably not produce vigorous and numerous children. If they did, it would simply prove that such work did not hurt them. There is no fear to be wasted on the danger of women's choosing wrong professions, when they are free to choose. Many women would continue to prefer the very kinds of work which they are doing now, in the new and higher methods of execution. Even cleaning, rightly understood and practised, is a useful, and therefore honorable, profession. It has been amusing heretofore to see how this least desirable of labors has been so innocently held to be woman's natural duty. It is woman, the dainty, the beautiful, the beloved wife and revered mother, who has by common consent been expected to do the chamber-work and scullery work of the world. All that is basest and foulest she in the last instance must handle and remove. Grease, ashes, dust, foul linen, and sooty ironware,—among these her days must pass. As we socialize our functions, this passes from her hands into those of man. The city's cleaning is his work. And even in our houses the professional cleaner is more and more frequently a man.

The organization of household industries will simplify and centralize its cleaning processes, allowing of many mechanical conveniences and the application of scientific skill and thoroughness. We shall be cleaner than we ever were before. There will be less work to do, and far better means of doing it. The daily needs of a well-plumbed house could be met easily by each individual in his or her own room or by one who liked to do such work; and the labor less frequently required would be furnished by an expert, who would clean one home after another with the swift skill of training and experience. The home would cease to be to us a workshop or a museum, and would become far more the personal expression of its occupants—the place of peace and rest, of love and privacy—than it can be in its present condition of arrested industrial development. And woman will fill her place in those industries with far better results than are now provided by her ceaseless struggles, her conscientious devotion, her pathetic ignorance and inefficiency.

3   FROM   *Margaret Sanger*
                    Birth Control

Until the twentieth century, the price asked of women who wished to escape from the economic dependency described by Gilman was high. Until reasonably effective birth control became available, women in effect were forced to choose between chastity and children, and the woman who wished to devote herself to a career was able to do so only by denying her own sexuality. A surprisingly high percentage of the first women college graduates remained single, giving rise to popular fears that educating women weakened the nation by preventing the brightest women from reproducing themselves.

Margaret Sanger (1883–1966) devoted much of her life to making birth control available to women. Although her clinics were frequently closed down by the police for violating state and federal laws declaring birth control devices and information obscene or illegal, she was responsible for bringing a hitherto prohibited subject to public attention.

SOURCE: Margaret Sanger, "Birth Control," *Woman and the New Race*, Truth Publishing Co., 1920, pp. 93–100. Reprinted by permission of Coward, McCann, & Geoghegan, Inc., from *Woman and the New Race*, by Margaret Sanger. Copyright 1920, by Brentano's, renewed 1948 by Margaret Sanger.

The problem of birth control has arisen directly from the effort of the feminine spirit to free itself from bondage. Woman herself has wrought that bondage through her reproductive powers and while enslaving herself has enslaved the world. The physical suffering to be relieved is chiefly woman's. Hers, too, is the love life that dies first under the blight of too prolific breeding. Within her is wrapped up the future of the race—it is hers to make or mar. All of these considerations point unmistakably to one fact— it is woman's duty as well as her privilege to lay hold of the means of freedom. Whatever men may do, she cannot escape the responsibility. For ages she has been deprived of the opportunity to meet this obligation. She is now emerging from her helplessness. Even as no one can share the suffering of the overburdened mother, so no one can do this work for her. Others may help, but she and she alone can free herself.

The basic freedom of the world is woman's freedom. A free race cannot be born of slave mothers. A woman enchained cannot choose but give a measure of that bondage to her sons and daughters. No woman can call herself free who does not own and control her body. No woman can call herself free until she can choose consciously whether she will or will not be a mother.

It does not greatly alter the case that some women call themselves free because they earn their own livings, while others profess freedom because they defy the conventions of sex relationship. She who earns her own living gains a sort of freedom that is not to be undervalued, but in quality and in quantity it is of little account beside the untrammeled choice of mating or not mating, of being a mother or not being a mother. She gains food and clothing and shelter, at least, without submitting to the charity of her companion, but the earning of her own living does not give her the development of her inner sex urge, far deeper and more powerful in its outworkings than any of these externals. In order to have that development, she must still meet and solve the problems of motherhood.

With the so-called "free" woman, who chooses a mate in defiance of convention, freedom is largely a question of character and audacity. If she does attain to an unrestricted choice of a mate, she is still in a position to be enslaved through her reproductive powers. Indeed, the pressure of law and custom upon the woman not legally married is likely to make her more of a slave than the woman fortunate enough to marry the man of her choice.

Look at it from any standpoint you will, suggest any solution you will, conventional or unconventional, sanctioned by law or in defiance of law, woman is in the same position, fundamentally, until she is able to determine for herself whether she will be a mother and to fix the number of her offspring. This unavoidable situation is alone enough to make birth control, first of all, a woman's problem. On the very face of the matter, voluntary motherhood is chiefly the concern of the woman.

It is persistently urged, however, that since sex expression is the act of two, the responsibility of controlling the results should not be placed upon woman alone. Is it fair, it is asked, to give her, instead of the man, the task of protecting herself when she is, perhaps, less rugged in physique than her mate, and has, at all events, the normal, periodic inconveniences of her sex?

We must examine this phase of her problem in two lights— that of the ideal, and of the conditions working toward the ideal. In an ideal society, no doubt, birth control would become the concern of the man as well as the woman. The hard, inescapable fact which we encounter to-day is that man has not only refused any such responsibility, but has individually and collectively sought to prevent woman from obtaining knowledge by which she could assume this responsibility for herself. She is still in the position of a dependent to-day because her mate has refused to consider her as an individual apart from his needs. She is still bound because she has in the past left the solution of the problem to him. Having left it to him, she finds that instead of rights, she has only such privileges as she has gained by petitioning, coaxing and cozening. Having left it to him, she is exploited, driven and enslaved to his desires.

While it is true that he suffers many evils as the consequence of this situation, she suffers vastly more. While it is true that he should be awakened to the cause of these evils, we know that they come home to her with crushing force every day. It is she who has the long burden of carrying, bearing and rearing the un-wanted children. It is she who must watch beside the beds of pain where lie the babies who suffer because they have come into overcrowded homes. It is her heart that the sight of the deformed, the subnormal, the undernourished, the overworked child smites

first and oftenest and hardest. It is *her* love life that dies first in
the fear of undesired pregnancy. It is her opportunity for self
expression that perishes first and most hopelessly because of it.
Conditions, rather than theories, facts, rather than dreams, gov-
ern the problem. They place it squarely upon the shoulders of
woman. She has learned that whatever the moral responsibility
of the man in this direction may be, he does not discharge it.
She has learned that, lovable and considerate as the individual
husband may be, she has nothing to expect from men in the mass,
when they make laws and decree customs. She knows that regardless of what ought to be, the brutal unavoidable fact is that she
will never receive her freedom until she takes it for herself.

Having learned this much, she has yet something more to
learn. Women are too much inclined to follow in the footsteps
of men, to try to think as men think, to try to solve the general
problems of life as men solve them. If after attaining their freedom, women accept conditions in the spheres of government,
industry, art, morals and religion as they find them, they will be
but taking a leaf out of man's book. The woman is not needed
to do man's work. She is not needed to think man's thoughts.
She need not fear that the masculine mind, almost universally
dominant, will fail to take care of its own. Her mission is not to
enhance the masculine spirit, but to express the feminine; hers
is not to preserve a man-made world, but to create a human world
by the infusion of the feminine element into all of its activities.

Woman must not accept; she must challenge. She must not be
awed by that which has been built up around her; she must reverence that within her which struggles for expression. Her eyes
must be less upon what is and more clearly upon what should be.
She must listen only with a frankly questioning attitude to the
dogmatized opinions of man-made society. When she chooses her
new, free course of action, it must be in the light of her own
opinion—of her own intuition. Only so can she give play to the
feminine spirit. Only thus can she free her mate from the bondage which he wrought for himself when he wrought hers. Only
thus can she restore to him that of which he robbed himself in
restricting her. Only thus can she remake the world.

The world is, indeed, hers to remake, it is hers to build and to
recreate. Even as she has permitted the suppression of her own
feminine element and the consequent impoverishment of indus-

try, art, letters, science, morals, religions and social intercourse, so it is hers to enrich all these.

Woman must have her freedom—the fundamental freedom of choosing whether or not she shall be a mother and how many children she will have. Regardless of what man's attitude may be, that problem is hers—and before it can be his, it is hers alone.

She goes through the vale of death alone, each time a babe is born. As it is the right neither of man nor the state to coerce her into this ordeal, so it is her right to decide whether she will endure it. That right to decide imposes upon her the duty of clearing the way to knowledge by which she may make and carry out the decision.

Birth control is woman's problem. The quicker she accepts it as hers and hers alone, the quicker will society respect motherhood. The quicker, too, will the world be made a fit place for her children to live.

4   FROM   *Crystal Eastman*
                    The Status of Women

Although radical feminist groups, such as the Congressional Union, continued to agitate for the vote during World War I, the National American Woman Suffrage Association supported President Wilson and American entry, maintaining a low profile until after the peace. Radical groups organized the First Feminist Congress in March 1919 in an effort to revitalize the women's movement and, more important, to draw public attention to the restrictions still imposed on women. Crystal Eastman, one of the founders of the Congressional Union, in this statement to the Congress, which she helped to organize, succinctly covers the areas where women were repressed and restricted—a list that belies the suffragists' contention that freedom for women was within their grasp.

SOURCE: Crystal Eastman, "Feminism," *The Liberator*, May 1919, p. 37.

For two years the whole western world has been talking about freedom and democracy. Now that the war is over and it is possible to think calmly once more, we must examine these popular abstractions, and consider (especially here in America where the boasting has been loudest)—how much freedom and democracy we actually have. Above all it behooves women to determine frankly what their status is in this republic.—

Four-fifths of us are still denied the elementary political right of voting.

Only one woman has held a seat in the United States Congress.

Only twenty-one women are sitting in our 48 state legislatures.

With rare exceptions all the higher executive offices in both state and federal governments are, by law or rigid precedent, open only to men.

In only six states do women sit on juries.

With half a dozen exceptions in the lower courts, there are no women judges.

In all government work, federal, state, county and city,—(notoriously in public school teaching),—women are paid much less than men for the same work.

In private industry, where it is estimated that twelve million women are now employed, the wages of women both skilled and unskilled (except in a few trades) are on a scale of their own, materially lower than the wages of men, even at work where their productive capacity is equal or greater.

Most of the strong labor unions, except in trades where women are in the majority, still close their doors to women workers.

Marriage laws in many states (including the guardianship of children) are designed to perpetuate the economic dependence of a wife on her husband. And nothing has been done in this country by way of maternity insurance or by giving to a wife a legal right to a share of her husband's earnings in recognition of her services as houseworker and nurse, to modify that dependence. And the vital importance of potential economic independence has yet to become a recognized principle of modern education for girls.

Voluntary motherhood is an ideal unrealized in this country.

Women are still denied by law the right to that scientific knowledge necessary to control the size of their families, which means
that among the poor where the law is effective, marriage can become virtual slavery for women.

Laws, judges, courts, police, and social custom still disgrace,
punish and "regulate" the woman prostitute and leave uncen-
sured the man who trades with her,—though in case of all other
forbidden vices the buyer as well as the seller suffers if caught.

From this brief statement of facts it is fairly clear that women
in America today not only share the wholesale denial of civil liberty which came with the war and remains to bless our victory,
but carry a special burden of restrictive legislation and repressive
social custom,—(not in any way relieved by the war for freedom
nor affected by the two years' crusade of democratic eloquence)—
a burden which halts them in almost every field of endeavor, and
effectually marks them as an inferior class. This is stated without
any bitterness and with full recognition of the fact that women by
their passivity have made these things possible. But it is stated for
a purpose.

It is my hope that this first Woman's Freedom Conference, held
in New York City, will see the birth of a new spirit in American
women—a spirit of humane and intelligent self-interest—a spirit
of determined pride—which will lead them to declare:

*"We will not wait for the Social Revolution to bring us the
freedom we should have won in the 19th century."*

PART TWO

Unsolved Problems

In the years immediately following the extension of suffrage to women in 1920, feminist activists lobbied successfully for several laws affecting women. The Sheppard-Towner Maternity and Infancy Protection Act of 1921 provided for a federally subsidized program of prenatal and postnatal care and instruction. In 1922, Congress passed the Cable Act, which allowed American women who married foreign nationals to retain their American citizenship. These early gains encouraged some feminists who, like Carrie Chapman Catt (Reading 5), hoped that women's influence would lead to further progressive reforms.

Catt and other social feminists were to be disappointed. Further legislative gains dwindled, and none were made after 1925. Right-wing Red-baiting of feminist organizations, dissension among feminist groups over the Equal Rights Amendment and other issues, and conservative opposition to the expansion of women's rights beyond the franchise all contributed to a serious weakening of the power of organized women.

The apparent loss of support and energy in the 1920s may also have resulted from the predictable "morning-after" of a successful crusade. Further, the much-celebrated revolution in manners and morals of that decade probably obscured the limited nature of women's political and economic gains. Women certainly underestimated the strength of traditionalist opposition to women's rights, as well as the strength and importance of conventional female stereotypes. Anne Martin (Reading 6), an activist who ran for the Senate from Nevada in 1918, argued in 1925 that both feminists, by their jealous guardianship of women's issues, and male politicians, by their reluctance to share their power, were responsible for the limited impact of enfranchised women on American politics. Another critic, Florence Seabury (Reading 7), in an essay that has considerable relevance today, stated that women would not be able to make serious changes in their social, economic, or political positions until the traditional sex-role stereotypes had been eradicated. She saw, at the end of a decade of ostensible social liberation, no sign that such a process was underway; indeed, the traditional stereotypes seemed to be as strong as ever.

Even though the campaign for birth control led by Sanger and others was reasonably successful by the 1920s, the woman who tried to combine family life with a career faced serious problems. Some of these difficulties, stemming from the persistence of the traditional ideas Seabury described, involved public acceptance of female professionals. Others had to do with child rearing and housekeeping, and the need to develop a fair division of labor between husband and wife. One woman who examined some of these problems in a diary published in 1933 was Dr. Mabel Ulrich (Reading 8), whose good humor did not spare her open discrimination because of her sex, as well as personal frustration that was perhaps more difficult to accept. Ulrich's difficulties are still with us, as Pat Mainardi's essay (Reading 17 in Part Four) indicates.

5   FROM   *Carrie Chapman Catt*
            Wanted: A New Department

This selection comes from the period of high hopes and early success after 1920. Carrie Chapman Catt, former president of the National American Woman Suffrage Association, calls for the establishment of a federal department of health, education, and welfare, at Cabinet level. (That department was finally established by President Eisenhower.) The editorial, which appeared in The Woman Citizen, *a suffragist journal which carried the slogan, "A Weekly Chronicle of Progress," suggests some of the interests of organized women.*

When Mr. Harding announced to his Marion visitors on Social Justice Day that he intended to create a new Cabinet Department under which social welfare was to be fostered, it was a new idea to most readers. Numerous interviews and publicity announcements have since made clear that the intention is not to establish a wholly new department, but to remove some of the bureaus now overtaxing the capacity of the existing Departments and to combine them under a new head, with the possible addition of new

SOURCE: Carrie Chapman Catt, "Wanted: A New Department," *Woman Citizen*, V, January 8, 1921, pp. 861–862.

features. Thus the Bureau of Education, now a minor factor in the big, crowded Department of the Interior, will become a part of the Public or Social Welfare Department. The Children's Bureau, which under Miss Lathrop's able management since its inception some ten years ago, has established its usefulness, and the Bureau of Health, will go into the new Department. These are the chief bureaus which have been chosen to compose the proposed Public Welfare Department, although there may be other existing bureaus which may be added and still other bureaus which may be created as a part of it. The idea, it must be remembered, is one of reorganization rather than one of creation.

The reorganization is sadly needed and it is an undeniable step toward efficiency to remove all related bureaus which are now serving what is commonly called public welfare and to combine them into a new Department. It is eminently proper to recognize the importance and the dignity of the Department by creating a Cabinet position for its head. The British Cabinet has twenty ministers, ours only ten; we could reasonably add several more Secretaries of Departments with advantage to our country. If the new Department is not authorized by this Congress, Mr. Harding, President, will recommend it in his first message to Congress, and the Republican majority will quickly translate the recommendation into law. So far, good; everyone approves.

In the distance, however, a rumble of dissatisfaction is heard. It is said that the doctors believing health, which is their specialty, to be the most important thing in the Department, are urging that the Health Bureau be the dominating factor with a doctor at the head of the combined Department. For some years the National Educational Association, composed of college presidents and faculties, normal and public school superintendents, principals and teachers, has been agitating for the promotion of the Bureau of Education to a Government Department with a Secretary of Education in the Cabinet. Educators now see their justifiable aim slipping farther away than ever, with the present bureau merely transferred to another Department but with no new dignity added. The head will be the chief of a bureau under a Secretary of Public Welfare instead of the Secretary of the Interior; that will be the only difference. Educators see their plea that more national recognition be given to education flouted and ignored, and are unhappy over it.

A conflict of ideas is therefore stirring among the adherents of these two bureaus of public welfare. The educators seem to us to have the best of it.

No government "of the people" can be safely administered by an ignorant electorate. Education is fundamentally necessary to the common welfare. Every man or woman voter who does not know the meaning of government by majorities, why citizens of a republic vote and what they can achieve with their votes, is a solid block to progress.

When the draft revealed that of 2,400,000 men between the ages of 21 and 31, more than 700,000 could not read and write, it was a challenge to our government to do something; something big and strong. We can afford no such conditions in this republic. Our national aim should be an electorate which speaks English and can read understandingly its own ballot. If we shall ever attain that aim the Federal Government must take the lead, hold aloft that standard and do it insistently every day in the year. Every party and every administration must do it.

Results commensurate to the need will not come forth from a little bureau whose chief is not the official equal of the Secretaries of Commerce, or Agriculture, or Labor.

Should this government send a commission to investigate and report upon educational systems in other progressive nations, the commission would be received and aided by Cabinet Ministers in Great Britain, France, Italy, Denmark, Norway, Sweden, Finland, Greece, The Netherlands, Spain and Japan. That is, the commission would be recognized as dealing with a subject elevated to an equal standing and equal governmental responsibility with war and commerce.

If any of those nations send a similar commission to this country, as many of them actually have done, they find the subject unrepresented in the President's Cabinet and the bureau an unimportant adjunct of a Department which was created chiefly to look after Indians. They find the Bureau of Education huddled into an inconspicuous corner where it holds an equal position with the Bureau of Indian Affairs, Bureau of Pensions, Bureau of

Patents, the General Land Office, Geological Survey, Reclamation
Service, National Park Service and the Bureau of Mines. The
chiefs of three of these bureaus, although in the same Department,
draw a considerably higher salary than the Chief of Education,
whose salary is $5,000. The highest salary is that of the chief of
the Reclamation Service, which is $7,500. The salary of Cabinet
officers is $12,000.

American orators on Fourth of July occasions speak of Education as the corner stone of our republic, the public schools as the
conservator of our most cherished ideals. With nearly three-
quarters of a million young men unable to read and write, and
Federal responsibility vested in a $5,000 chief of a bureau poorly
equipped, American Education proves to be altogether too rotten
a corner stone upon which to build a great republic.

Why not call the Department Education and Public Welfare?
Educators suggest thus lifting education to the position it merits.
The Deparment could carry as many bureaus as any other, but at
least we should have a Secretary of Education. If you think so,
sign the following coupon, cut it out and mail it to President-
elect Harding.

To Hon. Warren G. Harding,
    President-elect,
      Marion, Ohio.

    I beg you to recognize the importance of education in a
"government of the people" by naming the new Department
which you have so wisely proposed to create
       The Department of Education and Public Welfare.

        Name ....

        Street and Number ....

        City and State ....

6 FROM   *Anne Martin*

Feminists and Future Political Action

*Although organized feminists had campaigned for the passage
of the nineteenth amendment by emphasizing the beneficial political influence to be secured by extending the franchise to
women, and despite the early success of organized women in pass-
ing legislation favorable to women, women made only limited
gains after 1925. While the Women's Party tried to organize a
"feminist vote," working for the passage of the Equal Rights
Amendment first introduced in 1923, the larger League of Woman
Voters (organized by the National American Woman Suffrage
Association in 1920) generally adhered to a nonpartisan political
stance. In the following selection, Anne Martin, a Nevada feminist and candidate for U.S. Senator, makes an impassioned plea for
the revitalization of the women's movement around political action, describing the difficulties faced by activist women in the
1920s.*

Reflection on last fall's campaign and election leads me to this
conclusion: Either American feminists do not see the male dragons in their path, perception of which would compel a more
drastic attack to achieve their program of sex equality—or there
are no organized feminists in this country. Nothing else can explain the failure of woman's power to register effectively in the
Republican, Democratic, and La Follette campaign organizations,
or the melancholy feminist debacle of the election. The fact that
two women governors were elected, on conjugal and local issues,
and one member of Congress *not* the choice of the Woman's Party
in its belated campaign for a "woman's bloc" in Congress (all its
carefully selected candidates were defeated) reemphasizes this
failure.

SOURCE: Anne Martin, "Feminists and Future Political Action," *The Nation*,
February 18, 1925, pp. 185–186. Copyright *Nation*, 1921.

There is no doubt that Mrs. Carrie Chapman Catt sounded the doom of feminism for many years to come when she urged the newly enfranchised American women humbly to "train for citizenship," to join the men's parties, "to work with the party of your choice"—exactly where men political leaders wanted them, bound, gagged, divided, and delivered to the Republican and Democratic parties. This cataclysmic blunder led to the colossal futility of the League of Women Voters' "Get out the Vote" campaign in recent elections. Get out the vote? For what? For Harding or Cox; for Coolidge, Davis, or La Follette! Take your choice! —with the results that we see before us. But, I conclude hopefully, if Mrs. Catt should even now place a vital program of feminist issues before the women of the country, and a lively list of candidates, backed up if possible by the united power of women's organizations, there would be little trouble about "getting out the vote"—and in time electing many qualified women to public office, as a first concrete step toward "equality."

As for the Woman's Party, its hitherto inverted program of getting its "blanket bill" through the State legislatures and its equal-rights amendment through Congress by begging men legislators to do it for them, has only recently been turned right side up by its new policy of securing a "woman's bloc" in Congress. But I wonder if the quite general feeling that the Woman's Party puts its own advancement and aggrandizement ahead of the advancement of women as a whole is altogether unfounded. Does not its unconsciously childish attitude of jealous control over its own chosen issue, its assumed right of exclusive discovery and possession, stand in the way of sex solidarity, of genial *camaraderie* among women in the joyous adventure of winning sex equality? Undoubtedly, I conclude, this self-willed isolation short-circuits race currents of feeling, cut off from which no group movement can flourish. It accounts in part for the lack of vitality in the party's work, for the drying up of springs of enthusiasm for its (in some respects) excellent program.

As to the male dragons in the feminist path, the most formidable seems to be the behavior of men's political parties toward women, which must be described as follows: "The power (and the jobs) we have *we hold*." If women really want equality, must they not meet this male political behavior with a new kind of female

political behavior, must they not behave as human beings determined to develop in spite of a hostile environment have always
had to behave—must they not resist it, or be swamped by it, as
they were in the past election? Surely they must! . . .

Like all suppressed minorities in the political field, be they
labor, Hindu or Irish home rulers, Negroes or Pueblo Indians,
women will get only as much as they organize for and demand
effectually as a separate political force. Even if the La Follette
Party should develop greater enthusiasm for "equality" than it
has yet shown any sign of, it cannot achieve equality for women.
They must achieve it for themselves, and the straightest route
thereto is surely by way of sex solidarity in action—just as solid
as men's—expressed through the channels of women's organizations already existing, like the League of Women Voters and the
National Woman's Party. Can anything less secure the election of
qualified women, irrespective of party affiliations, to State legislatures and to Congress, on a fifty-fifty basis with men? Not until
existing political injustice against us whips us into united action
will equality be on the way. . . .

7   FROM   *Florence Guy Seabury*

                Stereotypes

*American women in the 1920s shed many of the restrictive con-
ventions of behavior that had characterized their activities in the
Victorian period. Manners changed quite dramatically as women
shortened their hair and their skirts, drank and smoked in public,
and began to recognize their own sexuality. Women continued to
make some occupational progress, moving in token numbers into
most professions. The flapper and the career girl were widely per-
ceived as new, emancipated women. However, despite the appar-*

SOURCE: Florence Guy Seabury, "Stereotypes," in *Our Changing Morality*,
Freda Kirchwey, Ed. (New York: A. and C. Boni, 1930), pp. 219–231. Copyright by A. and C. Boni, 1930.

*ent differences between the world of the flapper in the twenties
and that of the proper Victorian maiden, the changes in public
attitude necessary to release women from the restriction of female
stereotypes had not yet occurred. As Florence Guy Seabury points
out in the following selection, the same narrow definitions of
femininity and of woman's role that had confined the Gibson girl
applied to the flapper.*

If Clarissa Harlow could have stepped out of her pre-Victorian
world to witness some of the women stevedores and "longshore-
men" now at work along the New York water front, she would
certainly have fainted so abruptly that no masculine aid could
have restored consciousness. If we can believe the 1920 census, a
goodly number of Clarissa's timid and delicate sex are toiling
gloriously in the most dangerous and violent occupations. Nor
are they only engaged in handling steel beams and freight, running trucks and donkey engines, but as miners and steeplejacks,
aviators and divers, sheriffs and explorers—everything, in fact that
man ever did or thought of doing. They have proved, moreover,
as successful in such a new occupation as capturing jungle tigers
as in the old one of hunting husbands, as deft in managing big
business as in running a little household.

But the census bureau, compiling all the facts of feminine industry, forgot to note that woman might perform these amazingly
varied operations, outside the home, without changing in any
measurable degree the rooted conception of her nature and activities. She may step out of skirts into knickers, cut her hair in a
dozen short shapes and even beat a man in a prize fight, but old
ideas as to her place and qualities endure. She changes nothing
as set as the stereotyped image of her sex which has persisted
since Eve.

The Inquiring Reporter of the New York *Sun* recently asked
five persons whether they would prefer to be tried by a jury of
men or women. "Of men," cried they all—two women and three
men. "Women would be too likely to overlook the technical
points of the law." "Women are too sentimental." "They are too
easily swayed by an eloquent address." "Women are by nature

sentimental." Almost anybody could complete the list. . . . The status and attributes of women are settled by neat and handy generalizations, passed down from father to son, and mother to daughter. For so far, most women accept the patterns made for them and are as likely as not to consider themselves the weaker vessel, the more emotional sex, a lay figure of biological functioning. Optimists are heralding a changed state in the relationship of men and women. They point to modern activities and interests as evidence of a different position in the world. They say that customs and traditions of past days are yielding to something freer and finer. The old order, as far as home life is concerned, has been turned topsy-turvy. Out of this chaos, interpreters of the coming morality declare that already better and happier ways have been established between man and maid.

It sounds plausible enough, but the trouble remains, that, so far, it isn't true. The intimate relationship of men and women is about as it was in the days of Cleopatra or Xanthippe. The most brawny stevedorette leaves her freight in the air when the whistle blows and rushes home to husband as if she were his most sheltered possession. Following the tradition of the centuries, the business woman, whose salary may double that of her mate, hands him her pay envelope and asks permission to buy a new hat. Busts and bustles are out, flat chests and orthopedic shoes are in, while the waist line moves steadily toward the thigh—but what of it? Actualities of present days leave the ancient phantasies unchanged.

Current patterns for women, as formulated by the man in the street, by the movies, in the women's clubs and lecture halls can be boiled down to one general cut. Whatever she actually is or does, in the stereotype she is a creature specialized to function. The girl on the magazine cover is her symbol. She holds a mirror, a fan, a flower and—at Christmas—a baby. Without variety, activity, or individuality her sugary smile pictures satisfying femininity. Men are allowed diversity. Some are libertines, others are husbands; a few are lawyers, many are clerks. They wear no insignia of masculinity or badge of paternity and they are never expected to live up to being Man or Mankind. But every woman has the whole weight of formulated Womanhood upon her shoulders. Even in new times, she must carry forward the design of the ages.

One of the quaint hang-overs of the past is that men are the chief interpreters of even the modern woman. It may be that the conquest of varied fields and the strain of establishing the right to individuality has taken all her time and energy. Or it may be that the habit of vicarious expression has left her inarticulate. Whatever it is, in the voluminous literature of the changing order, from the earnest tracts on "How It Feels to Be a Woman," by a leading male educator to the tawdry and flippant syndicated views of W. L. George, masculine understanders take the lead. And the strange part of their interpretations is that they run true to ancient form. Old adages are put in a more racy vernacular, the X-ray is turned on with less delicacy, but when the froth of their engaging frankness disappears, hoary old ideas remain thickly in the tumbler. . . .

There may be men who are able to think of woman apart from the pattern of function, but they are inarticulate. Most of them spend their lives associating with a symbol. The set pieces they call Mary, Martha, Elaine, or Marguerite may follow the standardized design of grandmother, mother, or aunt. Or in more advanced circles, the pattern may call for bobbed hair, knickers, and cigarette case. Under any form of radicalism or conservatism the stereotype remains.

The old morality was built upon this body of folk-lore about women. Whether pictured as a chaste and beautiful angel, remote and untainted by life's realities, or more cynically regarded as a devil and the source of sin, the notion was always according to pattern. Naturally, the relationship of men and women has been built upon the design, and a great many of our social ideals and customs follow it. The angel concept led, of course, to the so-called double standard which provides for a class of Victorian dolls who personify goodness, while their sisters, the prostitutes, serve as sacrificial offerings to the wicked ways of men. The new morality, as yet rather nebulous and somewhat mythical, has fewer class distinctions. The angel picture, for instance, has had some rude blows. As portrayed by the vanguard of radicals and interpreters, however, the changing conventions have their roots in the old generalizations and phantasies.

Perhaps this is only to be expected, for the man or woman does not exist whose mind has not become so filled with accepted ideas of human beings and relationships before maturity, or even adolescence, that what is seen thereafter is chiefly a fog of creeds and patterns. If several hundred babies, children of good inherited backgrounds, could be brought up on an isolated island, without a taint of superimposed custom and never hearing generalizations about themselves—never having standardized characteristics laid heavily upon their shoulders, perhaps a different type of relationship founded upon actualities, would be evolved. Without a mythology of attributes, based chiefly upon biological functions, real human beings might discover each other and create new and honest ways of comradeship and association. As it is to-day, we do not know what the pristine reactions of individuals, free from the modifications of stereotype, would be like.

It was the development of means by which beliefs could be separated from actual facts which brought modern science into being and freed the world from the quaint superstitions of the ages. Not until the nature of substance could be proved and classified in contrast with the mass of ignorant notions which clogged ancient thought was the amazing mechanical, economic, and scientific advance of the last century possible. The world of antiquity had standardized life and tied thought down to speculative creeds. Empirical science discarded all supposition and centered itself upon building up another picture—life as an examination of its actual nature proved it to be.

In the creating of a new order which will bring with it a different type of social and personal contact, something similar must take place. For most of our ideas, even those classified as liberal and advanced, are built upon the reactions of an alleged, not an actual human being. Men have suffered from pattern-making, but never have they been burdened with the mass of generalizations that are heaped upon women from birth. Nobody knows what women are really like because our minds are so filled with the stereotype of Woman. And this picture, even in the interpretations of those who claim to understand the modern woman, is chiefly of function, not character. It is impossible to create a satisfying relationship between a red-blooded individual and a symbol. A changed morality cannot successfully emerge when half of those who participate are regarded not as people but functions. As long as women are pictured chiefly as wife, mother, courtesan

—or what not—defining merely a relationship to men—nothing new or strange or interesting is likely to happen. The old order is safe.

8   FROM   *Mabel S. Ulrich*

Diary

Some things have not changed. Women who step out of their conventional social role, today as in the early years of the century, face special problems, ranging from discrimination in employment to the difficulties of juggling familial and vocational responsibilities. Some of these problems are illustrated in the following excerpts from the diary of Dr. Mabel S. Ulrich, originally published in Scribner's *magazine in June 1933. The selections included here describe Dr. Ulrich's attempts to practice medicine and fulfill wifely functions, her efforts to start a college health service, and her service as a member of City Board of Charities supervising an urban hospital and health department. Ulrich's story illustrates the persistence of the stereotypes Seabury described in the preceding selection.*

April 4, 1904.

S. and I have decided to get married next year when we get through medicine. Of course we shall be fearfully poor at first, but as long as we are both going to work we shall make twice as much money as we could alone, and anyway we don't care. I told him I didn't know a thing about housekeeping, and he said why

SOURCE: Mabel S. Ulrich, "Men Are Queer That Way: Extracts From the Diary of an Apostate Woman Physician," *Scribners Magazine,* June 1933, pp. 365–369.

should I? That he could see no more reason for a woman's liking cooking and dishwashing than for a man's liking them. That since our education had been precisely similar, we are starting out exactly even, therefore there would be no justice at all in my having to do all the "dirty work"—although of course we both agree with Tolstoy that *all* manual work is honorable. So we have decided that one week I shall take over all the duties connected with the running of our house and the next week he will. Of course we are going to have an office together and be partners in every sense of the word. I was so happy I couldn't speak. Then after a long time we talked about our children. We are going to divide up the care of the children exactly as we divide the housework.

Sept. 23, 1905.

It is no go. We have given up the 50-50 housekeeping plan. We tried for a month but by the end of one week I knew. S. is a fearful mess as a housekeeper. Horribly expensive chops and steaks every day. Could *never* remember the laundry. Got furious if distracted Maggie called him at the office to ask what he wanted for dessert. And then of course he is busy and I am not. I have to laugh when I think how scared I was before we were married lest I might be the more successful at the start! Would he mind? I even asked him that, and he swore he would be proud. Well, you are perfectly safe, my dear S.! I have sat in that damned office for three months without a real call. Of course there are the hospital and dispensary, but I haven't made a cent. Today a woman came to the house and asked for the lady doctor. I was at the hospital but S. was in. Would she see him? Well—her little boy had broken his leg and she wanted the "lady" because she would be cheaper. When assured that the price would be the same she was delighted that after all she could have "a real doctor.". . .

April 19, 1915.

A Red Letter Day! Went over to our own University to present my college health plan to President S. He was a joy and seems even enthusiastically interested. We discussed the plan in detail and I believe it is going through. It was a great help to be able to say that the important ... U. had wanted me to try it out there! I am soaring.

April 25, 1915.

Prof. W. telephoned this morning that she thought my health plans were doomed because the President had heard I smoked cigarettes. I laughed and said she was crazy, but I rushed over to the campus just the same. And will you believe it, dear Diary, she was right! For the sake of my children's children let me put that conversation down as it transpired. This then, dear grandchildren, is how your grandmother and a president of a great university conversed in the Year of Our Lord 1915:

• *Your Grandmother, trying to smile quizzically:* I have been told that you have given up having me install my plan for health work because I smoke cigarettes.

• *President of a Great University, archly:* But you do, don't you?

• *Y. G., attempting puzzled amazement:* Yes, certainly, but what has that to do with it? Surely you do not think smoking a question of morals?

• *P. of G. U., hastily registering broadmindedness: I* don't, of course. But others know this about you too, and it is an undoubted fact that in the minds of most people a woman who smokes is—ah—confidently associated with—er—far more serious faults.

• *Y. G., frightened but gentle:* Do you honestly believe my plan to have value?

• *P. of G. U., indulgently:* I do.

• *Y. G., still gently:* Do you know any other person as well or better qualified to put it through?

• *P. of G. U., nervously:* No, I don't, but——

• *Y. G., triumphantly:* Well, then! You wouldn't deny this valuable opportunity to the students, merely because I smoke in my own house. I don't smoke in public, you know.

• *P. of G. U., looking at his finger nails, and becoming more and more presidential:* You have gained the reputation. We have very few women on our faculty, and they must be above suspicion.

Our regents demand this. It is even said that you have been
known to serve cocktails. (This he added with real reproach. I
laughed. I couldn't help it. A mistake.)

- *Y. G.:* Don't you ever drink anything, President S.?
- *P. of G. U., again impressively broadminded:* I used to enjoy
a glass of wine with my dinner when I lived in New York, but
since I have been President I have given up alcohol in any form.
As an example to——
- *Y. G., interrupting hopefully:* Yes, of course. Well, then, you
go to the Regents and say "Even as I used to drink wine and have
given it up, so this woman used to smoke cigarettes and has given
it up." For I will give it up—even if it does seem silly. Oh, President S., I do so want to try this out. I'll do it without any
pay—I——
- *P. of G. U., his presidential hand upraised:* It won't do. (A
long silence.)
- *Y. G.:* All because I'm a woman?
- *P. of G. U., solemnly:* Yes, but I want to know how sorry
I am.
- *Y. G., dreamily as she gathers up gloves:* When my mother
was a girl it was thought "fast" to use powder—positively immoral
to rouge.

Exit, leaving P. of G. U. booming a benediction.
So that, my dear grandchildren, although you will scarcely
believe it in 1940—is exactly that! . . .

Feb. 1, 1919.
Up betimes, to order meals, write school excuse note, explain
washing-machine to new laundress, and down to the Courthouse
for 8:30. First Board meeting. All seven of us eye each other and
try to take each other's measure. His Honor is President—bald,
whiskers, very bland blue eyes. Only four are his appointees. The
other two have been chosen by the City Council. We line up at
once. The Mayor's four all brotherly love, the others ready to
jump. All six men, however, unite in eyeing me with a certain
wariness and a this-damned-Woman's-vote expression. It is agreed
that each committee shall proceed to make a survey of its depart-

ment and bring in its report and recommendations. We adjourn, but remain for half an hour making tentative approaches. Was suddenly reminded of the way strange dogs, hair erect, but tails wagging, sniff each other before they commit themselves.
It's going to be great fun!

Feb. 16, 1919.

Worked all day on Health Department. Since I alone of my committee have any medical knowledge, they gladly leave all preliminary study to me. Department staff naturally enough united in antagonism to female investigator. Can't get many facts but sins of omission are there for any one to read. The entire place is archaic in organization, vital statistics, administration. But my word won't be enough. What I need is the Masculine Voice of Authority. A national voice, I think. . . .

March 10, 1922.

Now that Health Department and Hospital have been reorganized, there remains just one thing more I've set my heart on. We have got to make women graduates of the State Medical eligible for internship at the City Hospital. Had anticipated no trouble. After all it meant only that they be permitted to take a competitive examination. Today introduced subject for discussion. Was immediately opposed by every member! "If we let them take the examinations we will have only women in our hospital," said G. "The girls are always at the head of the class." Nobody but me thought that was funny. They all nodded their sympathy with G.
But this is not the end!

April 11, 1922.

Eureka! From this year on girls may compete for internship and two at least may hope to win! After all it wasn't so difficult. Preliminary tactics consisted of sowing fear in hearts of members. One woman from each women's organization of note was asked merely to call up each Board member, mention her group by name, and ask him how he intended to vote on the subject. That was all. Then this morning we saw to it that the Board room was packed with women. Each carried a pencil and pad *very* ostensibly, and very obviously intended for the record of votes. The prettiest and cleverest of the girl medics made an excellent speech, but it was hardly necessary. I asked that the vote be taken by name. The ladies busily scratched on their pads. There was only one dissenting voice. Thus ended the only occasion when pressure has seemed indicated. Usually the method is much simpler. If I want anything very much, I introduce the idea to a member, persuade him tactfully that the proposition in reality has sprung from his own brain—and let him do the rest. Not forgetting of course to encourage, admire, and applaud at frequent intervals. This policy of indirection, so contrary to lofty standards, was adopted after I found that my direct suggestions were met invariably by a suspicion six-male strong. . . .

June 17, 1924.

Home this morning after a week in New York. R. had in mind grand national job for me with salary of $10,000. But even L. couldn't swing it, and it fell through. Reason—the big salary. "They say," explained R. back from laboring for me in Washington, "they simply cannot afford to give a woman a job with that salary. You will find out, if you haven't already—that few men object to women holding jobs which pay up to $5000. But try beyond that! There's not a chance in a thousand."

And now? Steady! The important thing is not to feel beaten. Now is the time for all middle-aged (Yes, say it) women to come to the aid of their party. Woman's Club work? Charity? Volunteer lunch committees where fussy God-earnest gentlemen and graying ladies read reports and pass resolutions? No, I am through with that. Can a professional return happily to the amateur class? I doubt it.

Have decided to take the summer off and think it over!

PART THREE

Reaction: The Feminine Mystique

Despite the assaults of a generation of educated women seriously committed to careers, and an expansion of women into the labor force checked only temporarily by the Depression, the traditional stereotypes of woman's role continued to dominate American society. Feminists in the years after 1920 were attacked for trying to change the "natural" order, and America's failure to encourage women to fulfill their proper function was blamed for social problems ranging from juvenile delinquency to the high incidence of neurosis among young men conscripted to serve in the armed forces during World War II. For a time it became quite fashionable to attack the entire female sex, but especially dominating women, feminists, career women, and mothers, who were severely chastised by social critics for the havoc they had supposedly wrought on their husbands, children, and men in general (Reading 9).

While the Depression halted the growth of the female labor force, World War II provided a dramatic increase. Rosie the Riveter, the woman who replaced men sent into the armed forces, became something of a national heroine. Defense industries recruited working mothers by establishing day care centers. Because of the national emergency, the abandonment of the traditional female role became a patriotic duty. But once the war emergency ended, women's jobs were needed to provide occupation for the returning soldiers. The day-care centers closed, Rosie the Riveter was laid off, and women became once more an unused source of surplus labor. Not surprisingly, the traditional stereotypes were resurrected, buttressed with some Freudian theory, and used to encourage women to return to the family hearth, their "natural" sphere (Reading 10). Careers became suddenly unfashionable, and a generation of men and women who had struggled through depression and war as they reached maturity were only too glad to retreat into the security of private domesticity, encouraged by all the best authorities (Reading 13). What Betty Friedan has documented as the "feminine mystique" became the dominant popular theory regarding women.

In the pages of women's magazines, in college courses on marriage and the family, in fiction, in radio and television programs, the "feminine" woman was celebrated. The housewife and mother, using her intelligence and her creativity to bring new vigor to the traditional domestic role was glorified as the truly fulfilled woman. Feminism was unnatural, and the woman who chose a career in preference to an exclusive family-centered life was criticized for denying her own womanly nature (Reading 12).

Feminists, of course, did not passively accept the feminine mystique. Simone de Beauvoir's *The Second Sex*, published in 1953, during the height of the mystique, found an audience, although it was a small one. In this country, Ruth Herschberger published a stinging critique of contemporary attitudes toward women in 1948 (Reading 11). Despite the strength and coherence of these voices, they were soon drowned out by the supporters of the mystique. Women who dared to question the return to traditional patterns were warned by a host of authorities that they denied their own deepest instincts and threatened the happiness of their families by such challenges. Feminism had to wait for a general revival of reform in the 1960s for a resurgence of public interest.

9   FROM   *Phillip Wylie*
                            Common Women

Phillip Wylie's (1902–1971) fiercely antagonistic attack on "Momism" first appeared in 1942, as part of his Generation of Vipers, *which Wylie described as "a catalogue of what I felt to be wrong morally, spiritually and intellectually with my fellow citizens." According to Wylie, American women were raised to be impossibly romantic Cinderellas; once their girlhood was lost, they turned into selfish and destructive moms, who oppressed and corrupted husbands and children in the furtherance of their mindless selfishness. The suffragist campaign had been a step in the female takeover of American society. Wylie's attack coincided with a renewal of public concern over the "woman problem" and "Mom" became part of the language.*

. . . Mom got herself out of the nursery and the kitchen. She then got out of the house. She did not get out of the church, but, instead, got the stern stuff out of *it*, padded the guild room, and moved in more solidly than ever before. No longer either hesitant or reverent, because there was no cause for either attitude after

her purge, she swung the church by the tail as she swung everything else. In a preliminary test of strength, she also got herself
the vote and, although politics never interested her (unless she
was exceptionally naïve, a hairy foghorn, or a size forty scorpion),
the damage she forthwith did to society was so enormous and so
rapid that even the best men lost track of things. Mom's first gracious presence at the ballot-box was roughly concomitant with
the start toward a new all-time low in political scurviness, hood-
lumism, gangsterism, labor strife, monopolistic thuggery, moral
degeneration, civic corruption, smuggling, bribery, theft, murder,
homosexuality, drunkenness, financial depression, chaos and war.
Note that.

The degenerating era, however, marked new highs in the production of junk. Note that, also.

Mom, however, is a great little guy. Pulling pants onto her by
these words, let us look at mom.

She is a middle-aged puffin with an eye like a hawk that has just
seen a rabbit twitch far below. She is about twenty-five pounds
overweight, with no sprint, but sharp heels and a hard backhand
which she does not regard as a foul but a womanly defense. In a
thousand of her there is not sex appeal enough to budge a hermit
ten paces off a rock ledge. She none the less spends several hundred dollars a year on permanents and transformations, pomades,
cleansers, rouges, lipsticks, and the like—and fools nobody except
herself. If a man kisses her with any earnestness, it is time for mom
to feel for her pocketbook, and this occasionally does happen.

She smokes thirty cigarettes a day, chews gum, and consumes
tons of bonbons and petits fours. The shortening in the latter,
stripped from pigs, sheep and cattle, shortens mom. She plays
bridge with the stupid voracity of a hammerhead shark, which
cannot see what it is trying to gobble but never stops snapping its
jaws and roiling the waves with its tail. She drinks moderately,
which is to say, two or three cocktails before dinner every night
and a brandy and a couple of highballs afterward. She doesn't
count the two cocktails she takes before lunch when she lunches
out, which is every day she can. On Saturday nights, at the club
or in the juke joint, she loses count of her drinks and is liable to
get a little tiddly, which is to say, shot or blind. But it is her man
who worries about where to acquire the money while she worries

only about how to spend it, so he has the ulcers and colitis and she has the guts of a bear; she can get pretty stiff before she topples.

Her sports are all spectator sports.

She was graduated from high school or a "finishing" school or even a college in her distant past and made up for the unhappiness of compulsory education by sloughing all that she learned so completely that she could not pass the final examinations of a fifth grader. She reads the fiction in three women's magazines each month and occasionally skims through an article, which usually angers her so that she gets other moms to skim through it, and then they have a session on the subject over a canister of spiked coffee in order to damn the magazine, the editors, the author, and the silly girls who run about these days. She reads two or three motion-picture fan magazines also, and goes to the movies about two nights a week. If a picture does not coincide precisely with her attitude of the moment, she converses through all of it and so whiles away the time. She does not appear to be lecherous toward the moving photographs as men do, but that is because she is a realist and a little shy on imagination. However, if she gets to Hollywood and encounters the flesh-and-blood article known as a male star, she and her sister moms will run forward in a mob, wearing a joint expression that must make God rue his invention of bisexuality, and tear the man's clothes from his body, yea, verily, down to his B.V.D.'s.

Mom is organization-minded. Organizations, she has happily discovered, are intimidating to all men, not just to mere men. They frighten politicians to sniveling servility and they terrify pastors; they bother bank presidents and they pulverize school boards. Mom has many such organizations, the real purpose of which is to compel an abject compliance of her environs to her personal desires. With these associations and committees she has double parking ignored, for example. With them she drives out of the town and the state, if possible, all young harlots and all proprietors of places where "questionable" young women (though why they are called that—being of all women the least in question) could possibly foregather, not because she competes with such creatures but because she contrasts so unfavorably with them. With her clubs (a solid term!) she causes bus lines to run where they are convenient for her rather than for workers, plants flowers in sordid spots that would do better with sanitation, snaps independent men out of office and replaces them with clammy castrates, throws prodigious fairs and parties for charity and gives the proceeds, usually about eight dollars, to the janitor to buy the committee some beer for its headache on the morning after, and builds clubhouses for the entertainment of soldiers where she succeeds in persuading thousands of them that they are momsick and would rather talk to her than take Betty into the shrubs. All this, of course, is considered social service, charity, care of the poor, civic reform, patriotism, and self-sacrifice. . . .

It can be pointed out—and has, indeed, been pointed out before, though not, so far as I know, by any chap who has had such diverse and intimate contacts with the moms as I—that they are taking over the male functions and interpreting those functions in female terms. When the mothers built up their pyramid of perquisite and required reverence in order to get at the checkbook, and so took over the schools (into which they have put gelding moms), churches, stores, and mass production (which included, of course, the railroads, boats, and airplanes and, through advertising, the radio and the magazines), they donned the breeches of Uncle Sam. To this inversion I shall refer again. Note it.

I have explained how the moms turned Cinderellaism to their advantage and I have explained that women possess some eighty per cent of the nation's money (the crystal form of its energy) and I need only allude, I think, to the statistical reviews which show that the women are the spenders, wherefore the controlling consumers of nearly all we make with our machines. The steel puddler in Pittsburgh may not think of himself as a feminine tool, but he is really only getting a Chevrolet ready for mom to drive through a garden wall. I should round out this picture of America existing for mom with one or two more details, such as annual increase in the depth of padding in vehicles over the past thirty years due to the fact that a fat rump is more easily irritated than a lean one, and the final essential detail of mom's main subjective preoccupation, which is listening to the radio. . . .

We must face the dynasty of the dames at once, deprive them of our pocketbooks when they waste the substance in them, and take back our dreams which, without the perfidious materialism of mom, were shaping up a new and braver world. We must drive roads to Rio and to Moscow and stop spending all our strength in the manufacture of girdles: it is time that mom's sag became known to the desperate public; we must plunge into our psyches and find out there, each for each, scientifically, about immortality and miracles. To do such deeds, we will first have to make the conquest of momism, which grew up from male default. Our society is too much an institution built to appease the rapacity of loving mothers. If that condition is an ineluctable experiment of nature, then we are the victims of a failure. But I do not think it is. Even while the regiments spell out "mom" on the parade grounds, I think mom's grip can be broken by private integrity. Even though, indeed, it is the moms who have made this war.

For, when the young men come back from the war, what then will they feel concerning mom and her works?

10   FROM
Marynia Farnham and *Ferdinand Lundberg*
The Reconstruction of the Home

One version of popularized Freudian theory used to persuade wartime working women to return to the joys of domesticity was provided by Marynia Farnham and Ferdinand Lundberg in their bestselling critique, Modern Woman: The Lost Sex. *Spreading Freud's dictum, "anatomy is destiny," Farnham and Lundberg argued that the differences between men and women mandated their assignment to different spheres. Like Wylie, they argued that the high rate of neurosis in wartime draftees stemmed from*

SOURCE: From Ferdinand Lundberg and Marynia F. Farnham, M.D., *Modern Woman: The Lost Sex*, pp. 363–366 and 370–371, Copyright 1947 by Ferdinand Lundberg and Marynia F. Farnham. Reprinted by permission of Harper & Row, Publishers, Inc.

their maladjusted mothers. Going further, they suggested that most social problems, from mental illness to juvenile delinquency, could be traced to woman's failure to fulfill her proper social role. The glorification of the traditional female domestic role that Farnham and Lundberg prescribed for American women provides a clear example of the thinking behind the feminine mystique.

In order to get to the very roots of the problem—and the economic difficulties in raising children under the new machine order represent one of the roots—society must recognize that women, as much as men, need to feel useful, necessary, of real worth. In the past, generally speaking, women acquired these feelings through work and achievement within the circle of the home and family. Now, as we have seen, they do not. With the coming of industrial civilization, woman lost her sphere of creative nurture and either was catapulted out into the world to seek for achievement in the masculine sphere of exploit or was driven in upon herself as a lesser being. In either case she suffered psychologically.

What woman has lost must in some way be recaptured. Society must recognize her need and make it possible for her to satisfy her healthy ego aims without sacrificing her instinctive desire for motherhood or the needs of her children.

Government subsidies that would remove the economic pressure which forces many women to seek work outside the home is at least a step in the right direction. But a far more over-all attack is required. Furthermore, the problem is not only to get women into the home but to get them there on a basis satisfactory to their own feelings and aspirations. The Nazis got women back into the home; they ordered them there. But it is highly doubtful that the order accomplished more than to raise the birth rate, thereby adding to the multitude of obvious neurotics that was Germany of the Third Reich (and of the Weimar Republic and the preceding Second Reich).

If, however, women could be attracted into organizing their lives more closely around the home and spheres of nurture, an important step would have been taken in making the home a place where children might grow up into well-balanced adults. The home, clearly, cannot be constituted exactly as it was prior to the Industrial Revolution, even if this were desirable. But we believe it could be reconstituted on the older and more satisfactory emotional basis within the framework of a machine technology.

There are several courses it seems that might help to bring this about. In the first place, mothers should be given a large role in the formal education of children to the age of eighteen. As matters stand now, they have little part in the education of their children from kindergarten age onward. Education has, largely, been made into the monopoly of professional spinsters. Jobs teaching in school are still expressly reserved in most school districts as an economic perquisite of spinsterhood. Married women are widely barred by law or school board ruling from teaching. *We would suggest that this relic of a day when each county made this provision for its spinsters to keep them from becoming public charges be discarded and that all spinsters be barred by law from having anything to do with the teaching of children on the ground of theoretical (usually real) emotional incompetence. All public teaching posts now filled by women would be reserved not only for married women but for those with at least one child, with provision made for necessary exceptions.* The work day for each teacher would be reduced. More married mothers would be employed where now fewer unmarried women teachers are employed. There would be no reduction in the professional requirements of the teacher. Salaries would necessarily be reduced, but through the national mother's subsidy (operative even though the woman is employed and scaled only to the husband's earnings), there would be substantial restitution of the cut. Under such circumstances, of course, no woman teacher would earn so much as at present. As there are now about a million teachers in the United States (most of them women, most of them spinsters), there would be substantially more than a million married mothers employed as teachers, with considerable free time to devote to their own children and their households. They would be mothers with a sense of worth-while occupation, of being paid for their work, of being concretely recompensed for their children, of having free time for their children. They would be women, in short, with strong evidence before them of social concern for their lives.

What would happen to the spinsters? They would, perhaps, be encouraged to marry. If they did not, they would have to seek other jobs on the ground that they had not met the basic requirements, for this particular, vital employment. A great many children have unquestionably been damaged psychologically by the spinster teacher, who cannot be an adequate model of a complete woman either for boys or girls. In higher educational institutions, such as colleges, it does not matter so much, if at all. By that time the die has been cast.

(From time to time it may have appeared in these pages that we are freely prescribing marriage for all persons. But we are by no means doing this any more than we are prescribing childbearing. Too many people today are unfit for both activities for such a recommendation to make any sense.)

Mothers not seeking economic support should be encouraged to take part in the schoolwork both as assistants to the paid teachers and as students. There is much of value to the community that they could learn by attending school in special adult day classes, where they might study subjects of special interest to women: biology, child and male psychology, the history of women and the home, anthropology, dietetics, anatomy, physiology, chemistry, general medicine, nursing or problems in retail buying. Such classes could not fail to pay social dividends.

But all along the line it is the married mothers, rather than the spinsters and bachelors, who should be encouraged to superintend and administer the entire social process of rearing and educating children. Mothers should not be divorced from this important part of their job.

The principle of part-time work, already put into operation by a number of women, might be recognized as desirable for more married women. The gain from part-time employment would be that women at present devoting most of their time to work or career would be enabled to devote some of it to homes and children. A reciprocal gain would be that other women, who at present are engaged in nothing more important than afternoon bridge playing, would be induced to take up some socially and personally useful work on a half-time, paid basis. The quota of paid jobs for women might be doubled if there were a general resort to this pattern.

Another step toward re-establishing the home on a sound emotional basis would involve public recognition of the fact that the psychically balanced woman finds greatest satisfaction for her ego in nurturing activities. Teaching, nursing, doctoring, social service work, guidance, catering, decorating, play direction, furnishing, are all entirely feminine nurturing functions, and there are many others. There is almost unlimited room for expansion in some of these fields—for instance, social service work. In psychiatry, this work needs to be greatly expanded. . . .

It should be clear that we do not have in mind for women that anxiety-provoking bugaboo of the feminists: a lowly, inconspicuous role. On the contrary, we are suggesting a higher role than they have at present as poor imitators of men or as full-time slaveys in steam laundries, canning factories and so forth. As the domain we suggest for women broadly includes all of biology, psychology, sociology, medicine, pedagogy, philosophy, anthropology and several other systematic disciplines, it should be clear that there is ample room for women intellectually equipped for more technical achievement than their sisters. However, women who might nevertheless be inclined to enter fields belonging to the male area of exploit or authority—law, mathematics, physics, business, industry and technology—should certainly be allowed to do so.

Government and social-minded organizations should, however, through propaganda, make it clear that such pursuits are not generally desirable for women. Solely in the public interest, the disordered fantasies of the masculine-complex women should be combated in so far as those fantasies are advanced as the proper basis for public policy toward women as a whole. The emphasis of prestige, honor, subsidy and public respect should be shifted emphatically to those women recognized as serving society most fully as women. Discrimination all along the line should be shifted in their favor.

We propose that just as women should obtain status and prestige through motherhood, men should obtain it fundamentally by fatherhood. Bachelors of more than thirty, unless physically deficient, should be encouraged to undergo psychotherapy. They should also be subjected to differential tax rates so that they at least might enjoy no economic advantage over married men and fathers and might contribute to the social support of children. The bachelor, it might as well be recognized, is a dubious social quantity except in the fairly rare instances where he makes compensation by placing at the service of society some valuable skill. Most of them do not do this, and might just as well be bracketed in social esteem with the unmarried mother.

A program such as we have sketched, far from dividing men and women, would weld them closer together, would tend to make them complementary partners in a co-operative enterprise rather than competitors, as at present, in a jungle-like struggle with the child buffeted about in between. . . .

11   FROM   *Ruth Herschberger*
              A World of Differences

In 1948, Ruth Herschberger, poet and dramatist, published Adam's Rib, *a bitingly feminist analysis of the position of women in modern society. Even during the postwar heyday of the feminine mystique, feminists like Herschberger and, five years later, Simone de Beauvoir, in* The Second Sex, *continued the pattern established by Gilman and Goldman at the beginning of the century. In this selection from* Adam's Rib, *Herschberger explores sexual differences and their implications for society.*

"Man is a rational animal, but only women can have babies."

UNKNOWN

The history of mankind has been the search for some difference between individuals and groups of individuals—color, geo-

SOURCE: Ruth Herschberger, "A World of Differences," *Adam's Rib* (New York: Pellegrini & Cudahy, 1948). Copyright 1948 by Ruth Herschberger. Copyright © 1970 by Ruth Herschberger. Reprinted by permission of the author.

graphical location, sex—that would really count for something, a difference on the basis of which society could get organized, once and for all, and settle down to a peaceful senility. For some reason, the mere discovery of such a difference has meant that one group of people became subordinated to another group. And sooner or later the subordinate group would kick up a fuss.

The marked difference that distinguishes women from men is one of the most palpable differences to be found. It is women who have babies, men who cannot. Among legislative groups, in fact, women are sometimes regarded simply as the pregnant species. While only women can have babies, it must be remembered that they are not always having them. Women, during the childbearing period between adolescence and menopause, are not even fertile much of the time.

Dr. Dickinson has expressed it in this way, "The target, the ovum, is exposed only one-sixtieth of the time, a total of some seven whole days in the entire year, or a half-day thirteen times in that span. . . . As it is, Hartman declares that the difficulties in the way of conception are such that the human female should be classed actually as of low fertility."

Fertility is not a fixed condition in women, nor should it invariably be taken advantage of. The need for spacing children is recognized today, and consideration of the health of the mother is granted to be of some importance. Whether a given pregnancy will add a new life or transform existing children into orphans is no idle query. One-fourth of the maternal deaths in the United States occur unnecessarily, because the mothers are victims of chronic disease processes which make it impossible for them to survive pregnancy. Strangely enough, it is the over-idealization of the maternal instinct which accounts for thousands of neglected children among us.

HOW MUCH IS INSTINCT?

Science has sought to test in lower animals what it unromantically terms the maternal *drive*. A mother rat, it was found, will heroically cross an unpleasantly charged grill, receiving an electric shock, in order to rescue her helpless young on the other side.

But how long does her heroism persist? As E. C. Tolman, the psychologist, reports: "It varies in a predictable way with the age of the young, the state of the mammillary glands, and the like." When the young animals grow a bit older, the mother will no longer cross the electric grill to rescue her own flesh and blood, not even her favorite son that inherited its father's bead eyes.

The maternal instinct in humans is not predicated on the condition of the mammillary glands. The maternal instinct is a great and stimulating ideal because it comprises traits not so specifically maternal as human. The qualities we attribute to motherhood are basically human qualities; they include a warm regard for other persons, their needs and difficulties. That this entire complex of sympathy should today be subsumed under the maternal instinct, thus making "love" a female responsibility, helps account for the state of the world. The better factors afloat in maternalism—considerateness, generosity, protectiveness—are scarcely the temperamental monopoly of the female. Nor can women be called upon to establish international peace simply by exerting mother love in all directions; not while they continue to bring up their male children in a tradition that regards concern for other people's needs as unmanly.

The maternal instinct in women is frequently illustrated by an image of a tigress who defends her young against all threats, fiercely and, we like to think, successfully. We find equally prevalent a picture of motherhood typified by utter, or even abject, helplessness. As Havelock Ellis describes it, "In woman, the long period of pregnancy and lactation, and the prolonged helplessness of her child, render her for a considerable period of her life economically dependent."

Yet the tigress is not notably dependent during the prolonged helplessness of her young, and neither—come to think of it—is primitive or modern woman, who usually goes right on with her heavy housework a few weeks after childbirth. In fact, housework is often increased by the birth of a child. It is true that the woman has a protector, and that he goes off to the office every day where he sits quietly at a desk earning money. But the helpless young mother may be at home doing a washing that requires three times the muscular exertion he expends.

With the image of the protective tigress we satisfy ourselves that mother love is a sufficient antidote for poverty, chronic ill-health, or any injustice; while with the helplessness of mother-hood we enjoy the thought that a woman is throughout life dependent on man's good will and protection.

HOW DIFFERENT ARE DIFFERENCES?

That women can have babies and men cannot is a genuine difference between the sexes. Does this mean that the similarities between women are greater than their differences, and that these similarities are more important than any similarities they share with men? "Regardless of the social differences between women in different cultures or classes, from the primitive to the most civilized, and the most sophisticated to the most lowly," writes Amram Scheinfeld, "they share many vital experiences—the menstrual process, motherhood and their relationships to men—which bring them together in their thoughts, personality, and behavior."

The mere mention of vital experiences, as esoterically possessed by women, has heretofore silenced any tendency on the part of women to question the uniformity of those overwhelming deter-miners of character, menstruation and childbirth. To speak of vital experiences is like talking about love. No one really believes that love is the same for every individual, but the generalization is pleasant.

This stress on the joyous uniformity of women's subjective experiences has been made for the most part by men, who express at the same time their jealous inability to participate in these purely feminine experiences. It is the male author who so often tells us in detail why certain physiological processes, such as menstruation, are exercising a conclusive influence on our thoughts, personality, and behavior. Yet, speaking from their own premises, who is less qualified to judge these vital experi-ences than the sex which admits it has been excluded from them?

If women were asked what they actually thought about these shared experiences—whether they found them exciting, terrify-ing, tedious, expected or unexpected—society would be disillu-sioned by the diversity of the answers. Do women's "relationships

to men" really bring them closer together than their interest in
different men marks them apart? *What on earth can she see in
him!*

ON BEING OURSELVES

It seemed to Aristotle that man, as the one rational animal,
ought to stick to rationalizing. When man was not reasoning, he
became mere animal, vegetable, or mineral. Thanks to an enlarged forebrain, it was discovered that man of all beasts was
able to set up abstract standards of behavior uniquely capable
of embarrassing those who did not live up to them. Thus man
came to distinguish himself as the animal-with-symbols, the
idealist and the standard-bearer, as well as the most embarrassed.

In this development of the creative differences of man, as distinct from other fauna, two capabilities have been overlooked,
at least by philosophers. One of these is the erect carriage; man
is the only primate who makes even a sporting attempt to stand
up straight. Secondly, man is the only mammal with a thumb
opposite to his fingers.

When we look about us, we find that the aristocratic tradition
has indeed cultivated the erect carriage as the outstanding fea-
ture of man, leaning backward ever so slightly in order to show
a clear advance over the gibbons. Industrialists, on the other
hand, have developed the assembly line expressly to provide an
outlet for man's unique ability for grasping, nailing, hammering,
and other digital triumphs.

Perhaps it is these vital pinching-experiences which bring all
men together in their thoughts, personality, and behavior. The
chimpanzee may have a thumb, but it is not opposite to the
fingers. He can swing aimlessly from tree to tree, but is never
found settling down on the installment plan. For this requires a
pinching aptitude he does not possess, one only dimly fore-
shadowed in squirrels and other of the more prudent rodents.

From time to time man has gone mad with pride over his
uniquenesses, especially his difference from women and his difference from the other animals. In truth there is something
stirring about man's upright carriage. His infinite patience with

pinching together bits of machinery and small change is also noteworthy. Man's power of abstract thought is unexampled: his ability to subtract one reality from another and come out with something like the *Ding-an-sich* that smells and tastes realer than the original ingredients.

Yet there is no rule by which we must develop only what we have "uniquely" to offer (like a freak in the circus); we should be allowed an expression of choice as to which of our multiple capabilities we wish to exert. The progressive school with its admonition to "be creative" often has preconceptions of what the creative is to be. These premeditated potentialities are given a few years of grace in which to emerge, but if they have not come out of hiding by that time—back to the birch rod.

While women's ability to bear children is one of the most unique and impressive to be found, women are also rational animals with a pinching dexterity, an erect carriage, and certain other qualities. Must a woman cultivate only that uniqueness which distinguishes her from man (and links her with the animals), or is she to be allowed to exhibit some purely human characteristics as well?

If the human animal chooses on occasion to become a runner of marathons, we need not protest that he is bringing down on us the ridicule of all odd-toed ungulates, who also possess a faculty for running and a better one. Man may want to indulge his kinship with the animals at times, thus distinguishing himself from the motionless tomato and from the minerals who possess such alarming permanence. Human society would in any case be more pleasant to live with if man remembered more often that he is the only laughing animal.

12   FROM   *Life*

Modern Marriage

Despite the efforts of women like Herschberger who tried to keep the ideas of feminism alive, those ideas were overshadowed by the vision of domesticity in the postwar era. Social critics, distressed by a rising divorce rate, sought to explain the failure of so many marriages in terms of the inability of women to comprehend and fulfill their proper role in the family. In this selection from Life *magazine's special issue "The American Woman" (1956), five psychiatrists from different regions of the nation provide an explanation for family difficulties in classic mystique terms.*

DIFFERING EMOTIONAL NEEDS

Men are designed by nature to sire children and women to bear them, and from these elementary facts, psychiatrists say, come their differences in emotional needs. For women, the sexual act itself implies receptiveness and a certain passivity, while the long period of human gestation and the extraordinarily long period of a child's dependence implies a need for protection and support for the mother. These primary feminine qualities— receptivity, passivity and the desire to nurture—color a woman's entire emotional life.

For the male, the sexual role requires aggressiveness and a certain degree of dominance, even of exploitiveness (the desire to utilize others for one's own advantage). These male characteristics are carried into everyday living in many ways. Since the male's primary function is simply to impregnate he can feel somewhat detached from the result; yet one of the significant ways in which male humans differ from, say, male monkeys is

SOURCE: Robert Coughlan, "Changing Roles in Modern Marriage," *LIFE*, December 24, 1956. Robert Coughlan, LIFE Magazine, Copyright © 1956, Time, Inc. Reprinted with permission.

that male humans in every society provide for their females and their young. To be a man, therefore, carries with it not only the qualities mentioned above but the idea of responsibility. And it is precisely at this fundamental level, the psychiatrists fear, that the general trend of American society is unhealthy. Spottily and sporadically, but increasingly, the sexes in this country are losing their identities. The emerging American woman tends to be assertive and exploitive. The emerging American man tends to be passive and irresponsible. As a result neither sex can give to nor derive from marriage the satisfactions peculiarly necessary to each. They are suffering from what the psychiatrists call sexual ambiguity.

THE PIONEER TRADITION

This is not a peculiarly American disease but it is more prevalent here than any place else in the world, and the reasons are embedded in some of the very factors that made the nation great. As a pioneer society, we attracted and bred people who were resourceful and had a well-founded sense of their own importance. The members of the pioneer family were deeply interdependent. The father built the home and raised the crops; the mother cooked the food and raised the children. There could be no lack of what the psychiatrist calls "ego-supporting roles." Then came the industrial revolution and the same energetic qualities that had conquered the wilderness produced an abrupt and explosive transformation of our way of life. From a predominantly rural and agricultural society we rapidly became a predominantly urban and industrial one. This had an unsettling effect on the emotional lives of both men and women, but particularly women.

Why particularly women? Because, the psychiatrists believe, the sudden change destroyed the traditional basis for woman's self-respect, her sense of her own value to society. Her husband now was away at an office or factory, out of sight and doing things from which she felt detached. Children became an economic burden instead of an economic asset. The home itself, the center of her deepest emotional satisfactions, lost not only its economic value but most of the educational and recreational ones she had supervised. Worst of all, the men, with their new orientation toward money-making skills, began in effect to patronize women. Women were pets, housekeepers, sometime companions, mistresses, biological mechanisms to produce a child or two. But, except where the older patterns persisted, they were no longer important in their own right.

Naturally women reacted, and their most conspicuous reaction took the form of "feminism," a supercharged political movement which had as its goal "equality between the sexes." Women demanded their "rights." Since males seemed to be having much the best out of life, the male criteria became the feminist goal. "Rights" were what men had, legally, socially and morally. Thus the idea that women should be "as good as" men soon became transposed into the idea that women are really "the same as" men, saving only a few anatomical details, and that what is good for one sex is equally good for the other.

"Feminism" as such became moribund after women received the right to vote and it now seems as quaint as linen dusters and high button shoes. But it yielded one major product, that common urban phenomenon known as the "career woman." And the fatal error that feminism propagated sank deeply into the national consciousness. It has cost both sexes dearly. To count those costs, and to see where and how they occur, it is best to turn to the panel members who deal with them in their daily encounters with emotionally wounded people.

In New York City the "career woman" can be seen in fullest bloom and it is not irrelevant that New York City also has the greatest concentration of psychiatrists. These women are a subject of special interest to Dr. John Cotton. Their marriages, he finds, are characterized by certain similarities or common symptoms—a pattern which might be called the New York Career Woman "syndrome."

At the center of this syndrome one finds a bright, well-educated, ambitious wife, probably in her mid-30s, well-dressed and attractive. She and her husband both work and make about the same amount of money—around $10,000 a year each. They live well and can afford a servant to run the home and look after the one or two children. Everything seems to be wonderful.

THE WIFE SEEKS HELP

Then, one day, the wife (it is almost always the wife) arrives at the psychiatrist's office for advice about her marriage. Her husband is drinking too much, she says. He doesn't take on his share of responsibilities, whether it be writing the checks for the monthly bills or seeing about vacation reservations. He is not aggressive sexually; in fact he often seems indifferent to her. When they do have relations, she finds it difficult to get satisfaction. They quarrel a good deal, and one or two times, when he has been drinking, he has actually hit her. She has lost a lot of her respect for him. She doesn't want to be a clinging vine, goodness knows, but at least she wants a man she can depend on. Someone who does the things a man is supposed to do. A *man*.

Enter now the husband. He drinks a bit more than is good for him, he agrees, and does things he is sorry for later. The marriage is not in good shape. But the trouble with his wife is that she tries to run everything. She has strong ideas and he . . . well, rather than get into a wrangle he had tried to see things from her point of view, and finally began letting her make most of the decisions. He was sexually attracted to his wife and still thinks she is a good-looking woman. But she expects him to respond to her mood. She is independent and assertive in all their other relationships, and then suddenly she switches to the role of yielding seductress; he cannot make the transition. He admires her as a person but does not think she is much of a wife. She dislikes housework, she never learned how to cook, she turned the children over to nurses as soon as she could. She gives them presents but doesn't give much of herself to them. She never gives much of herself to *him*. He wishes she would do more of the things that women are supposed to do. He wishes she were more of a *woman*.

How did these two people get into this fix? Cause and effect are seldom clear cut in the human personality, since the hereditary and environmental factors that form a single individual are almost infinitely variable. But a specialist like Dr. Cotton can trace the most probable sequence of events.

The wife may well have been raised in a household in which the mother directly or indirectly rejected her own female role.

Directly, perhaps, by choosing to go to work outside the home. Indirectly, perhaps, by her sense of dissatisfaction at staying home, reflected in remarks about the dullness of housework, the trials of giving birth and of being a mother and so on. At the same time, the mother probably was the dominant personality in the household, with the father a somewhat shadowy figure in the minds of the children—shadowy because he was unassertive or uninterested or, more likely, simply because his job kept him away all day and brought him home at night too late and too tired to spend time with them.

The little girl, then, very early formed the idea that womanly occupations are unpleasant. She grew up in a culture that put a higher value on getting and spending than on conceiving and bearing. So she was naturally inclined toward a career, toward independence, toward "self-expression." As she moved ahead in her career, she would of necessity develop those sides of herself that were most aggressive. She might well mask these under a feminine manner. But one way or another she would acquire attitudes of aggression, exploitation and dominance, and to that degree would become masculinized. And this charatcer she would take into marriage.

Why would she marry? Partly for sexual gratification, which she would consider an inalienable "right." But also because she would still be basically a woman, driven by her primitive biological urge toward reproduction, toward homemaking and nurturing. And however much she might scoff at the idea intellectually (being "independent"), she would deeply want to be able to submit to her husband, to find in him the essential male qualities which would complement her essential female ones. Yet the chances would be against her finding them. The chances would be, because of her masculine-aggressive character, that she would unconsciously pick out a man who could be dominated. Where would he come from?

He might well come from an emotional environment rather similar to her own, one, that is, in which the mother was the dominant figure in the child's eyes and in which she somehow rejected her feminine role. The boy, needing his mother's love, tried to please her. And in manner and form he may have succeeded, for such women often overcompensate for their guilty feelings of dissatisfaction by becoming overprotective, overaffectionate or dominating mothers. In either case his orientation was toward pleasing mother and he was likely to feel dependent on her in many ways, especially to the degree that he lacked a strong and available father image on which to pattern himself. When he became a man and married he probably brought with him a passive attitude and began to look to his wife for protectiveness, praise, the feeling that she was looking out for him.

Yet his basic maleness is still there and he wants a wife who will let him assert it. If she does not, he is wounded at the deepest levels of his ego and reacts unpleasantly.

Thus we have the syndrome in its essence: each partner brings to the marriage mutually contradictory wishes. She brings the wish to dominate and to be dominated, and he brings the wish to be passive and to be aggressive.

On the face of it the case history just related is an unusual situation, for how many "career women" wives make $10,000 a year? Then why bring it up? It is brought up because it illustrates in extreme form a general problem which Dr. Cotton observes at many social and economic levels in New York. It can be transposed to the suburbs, where the great majority of wives do not have "careers."

"JUST A HOUSEWIFE"

If there is such a thing as a "suburban syndrome," it might take this form: the wife, having worked before marriage, or at least having been educated and socially conditioned toward the idea that work (preferably some kind of intellectual work, in an office, among men) carries prestige, finds herself in the lamentable position of being "just a housewife." To be "just a housewife" is to be degraded: she announces her position to the census taker with an apologetic flinch. In the circumstances in which many young-marrieds find themselves—a cramped house or apartment, two or three small children needing constant attention, no money for servants or luxuries—she may become morbidly depressed.

If she avoids depression or recovers from it, observes Dr. Cotton, her humiliation still seeks an outlet. This may take various forms: in destructive gossip about other women, in raising hell at the P.T.A., in becoming a dominating mother who supervises every detail of her children's lives, or above all in dominating her husband, that undeservedly fortunate creature who gets to travel to the city every day and engage in those interesting business activities which she envies. In her disgruntlement she can work as much damage on the lives of her husband and children (and her own life) as if she were a career woman, and indeed sometimes more.

The pattern can be transposed to the lower economic level of the factory wife. She works, she almost always says, because she wants to buy something for the home, or to give her children a better education than she had, or for some other rationally satisfying reason. And indeed there are multitudes of pressures to make her do so, for the whole idea of progress and self-betterment, the very driving force of American society, is manifested in more and better automobiles, refrigerators and television sets, and in more and better education.

On the other hand, a great many factory wives work because, deep down, the wife-mother-homemaker role bores them and they get a greater sense of importance by entering a male environment. In any case, the result for the factory wife is similar to that among the suburban and "career" wives. If she does not work she feels degraded, and if she does work she may begin to take on masculine attitudes. The factory couple, leaving perhaps on the same bus in the morning, both perhaps wearing trousers, he soldering the radio parts which she later puts together on an assembly line, coming home equally tired to their frozen-food ready-cooked dinners and the television set they have bought with their joint earnings, are sexually undifferentiated at all times except in the nuptial embrace. The relationship is mutually insulting to their primary maleness and femaleness.

One of the worst aspects of this general situation, Dr. Cotton points out, is that it tends to repeat itself in magnified form with each new generation. The masculinized mother and feminized father produce girls who are even more masculine, boys who are even more feminine. In his practice he has come upon a considerable increase in frigidity and impotence, and he has been especially struck by the increase in male homosexuality

13 FROM *Benjamin Spock*

The Common Sense Book of Baby and Child Care

During the years after World War II, the generation that had grown to maturity in an era of war and depression enjoyed considerable affluence. The growth of suburbia, a rising birth rate, and a diminished concern for social problems, including feminism, characterized middle-class America in the fifties, as its inhabitants seemed to retreat into the privacy of the nuclear family. The child-centered mother celebrated by the feminine mystique found guidance and direction in the work of Dr. Benjamin Spock (1903–   ).

The publication of Spock's Common Sense Book of Baby and Child Care *in 1946 marked a swing away from the rather rigid child-rearing methods of the behaviorists of an earlier generation who had promoted scheduling of infants and had warned parents not to spoil children with too much affection. Spock's more flexible approach, emphasizing the parents' needs and instincts, as well as those of the child, appealed to middle-class parents. Although Spock encouraged parents to follow their own instincts to find solutions that were comfortable for both parents and children, in many ways his advice reflects the social standards of his time. In the following selections, dealing with the emotional development of the child and with working mothers, Spock's approach is conservative, and quite consistent with the ideology of the feminine mystique.*

A Girl Needs a Friendly Father, Too. It's easy to see that a boy needs a father to pattern himself after, but many people don't realize that a friendly father plays a different but equally

SOURCE: Benjamin Spock, M.D. *The Common Sense Book of Baby and Child Care* (New York: Simon and Schuster, 1957). Copyright 1945, 1946 by Benjamin Spock, M.D. Reprinted by permission of Pocket Books, a division of Simon and Schuster, Inc. ⓒ 1957 ⓒ 1968 by Benjamin Spock, M.D.

important part in the development of a girl. She doesn't exactly pattern herself after him, but she gains confidence in herself as a girl and a woman from feeling his approval. I'm thinking of little things he can do, like complimenting her on her dress, or hair-do, or the cookies she's made. When she is older, he can show her that he's interested in her opinions and let her in on some of his. Later, when she has boy friends, it's important for him to welcome them, even if he secretly doesn't think they are quite good enough for her.

By learning to enjoy the qualities in her father that are particularly masculine, a girl is getting ready for her adult life in a world that is half made up of men. The way she makes friendships with boys and men later, the kind of man she eventually falls in love with, the kind of married life she makes, are all influenced strongly by the kind of relationship she has had with her father throughout her childhood. . . .

DEVOTION TO THE PARENTS

A Boy Now Wants To Be Like His Father.   By the age of 3 a boy is beginning to realize more clearly that he is a boy and will grow up to be a man like his father. This gives him a special admiration for his father and other men and boys. He watches them carefully and works hard to be as much like them as he can, in appearance and behavior and interests. In his play he concentrates on propelling toy trucks, trains, and planes, pretending his tricycle is a car, being a policeman or fireman, making deliveries, building houses and bridges. He copies his father's remarks in his father's tone of voice. He takes on his father's attitude toward other males and toward women. He is preparing himself to play a man's part in the world, spiritually, occupationally, socially, by means of his love and admiration of his father and other men.

A Girl Wants To Be Like Her Mother.   The girl at this age realizes that it is her destiny to be a woman, and this makes it particularly exciting and challenging for her to try to be like her mother and other women. She turns with more concentration to housework and baby (doll) care if these are her mother's occupations. In caring for her dolls, she takes on the very same attitudes and tone of voice her mother uses toward children. She absorbs her mother's point of view toward men and boys. . . .

THE WORKING MOTHER

To Work or Not To Work? Some mothers have to work to make a living. Usually their children turn out all right, because some reasonably good arrangement is made for their care. But others grow up neglected and maladjusted. It would save money in the end if the government paid a comfortable allowance to all mothers of young children who would otherwise be compelled to work. You can think of it this way: useful, well-adjusted citizens are the most valuable possessions a country has, and good mother care during early childhood is the surest way to produce them. It doesn't make sense to let mothers go to work making dresses in a factory or tapping typewriters in an office, and have them pay other people to do a poorer job of bringing up their children.

A few mothers, particularly those with professional training, feel that they must work because they wouldn't be happy otherwise. I wouldn't disagree if a mother felt strongly about it, provided she had an ideal arrangement for her children's care. After all, an unhappy mother can't bring up very happy children.

What about the mothers who don't absolutely have to work but would prefer to, either to supplement the family income or because they think they will be more satisfied and therefore get along better at home? That's harder to answer.

The important thing for a mother to realize is that the younger the child the more necessary it is for him to have a steady, loving person taking care of him. In most cases, the mother is the best one to give him this feeling of "belonging," safely and surely. She doesn't quit on the job, she doesn't turn against him, she isn't indifferent to him, she takes care of him always in the same familiar house. If a mother realizes clearly how vital this kind of care is to a small child, it may make it easier for her to decide that the extra money she might earn, or the satisfaction she might receive from an outside job, is not so important, after all.

PART FOUR

The New Feminism

The victory of the traditional model was not complete, however, and after a decade of glorified domesticity, disturbing indications that all was not well with the happy housewife began to appear. After a brief postwar decline, the number of working women began to increase, continuing a century-old pattern. Despite continued discrimination in salaries and in employment, lack of child-care facilities, and rather strident public criticism of working mothers, women continued to enter the world of work whenever they had the opportunity to do so. The increasing incidence of alcoholism and mental health problems among educated middle-class women in the suburbs began to reach public attention. As their children reached maturity and left home for college and careers, a generation of child-centered mothers was forced to seek out a new focus for life. In her best-selling book, *The Feminine Mystique*, Betty Friedan exposed the high social and psychological costs of the traditional female role. Her suggestions for change dealt primarily with the possibilities available for educated women who could involve themselves in interesting careers—the most visible and articulate of discontented women (Reading 15). At about the same time, a special Presidential Commission on the Status of Women, appointed by President John F. Kennedy at the beginning of his term of office, issued a report documenting the existence of widespread discrimination against women in employment, promotion, and salaries. Alice S. Rossi (Reading 14) called for changes in the position of women and debunked the theory that women had attained full emancipation after 1920. As public attention began to turn once more to battles supposedly fought and won before 1920, Friedan, in 1965, founded the National Organization of Women to work for equality.

The decade of the sixties was also the decade of the civil rights and antiwar movements. Young Americans left their comfortable homes to risk their lives in Southern voter-registration drives and, later, protested American involvement in the Vietnam conflict on college campuses, and in the streets of Berkeley, New York, and Washington. Many young women, committed to civil rights or antiwar organizations dedicated to freeing the oppressed and extending democratic principles, discovered that they, as women, were relegated to secondary positions in the struggle. When civil rights leader Stokeley Carmichael, head of the Student Nonviolent Coordinating Committee, heard the complaints of some women in his organization that they were not being given their fair share of power and prestige, he responded with the now celebrated remark: "The only position for women in SNCC is prone." In response to the lack of comprehension of the women's demands by the male leadership of SNCC and other organizations, women began to meet in small groups to discuss their problems and to plan action to improve their situations.

It is from these two strains, one reformist, one radical, that the present women's liberation movement descends. On some issues, for example, reform of abortion laws, reformists and radicals find it easy to cooperate for an immediate change that will bring some improvement to women's lives. On other issues, for example, the structure of male-female relationships, the two wings of the movement find it less easy to reach agreement, as radical feminists call for changes in the basic structure of society too drastic for reformists to support. Nationally organized groups like Friedan's NOW have concentrated on legal action, securing equal pay, fair employment practices, attempting to change laws that discriminate against women, and resurrecting the equal rights amendment to the Constitution after nearly half a century of neglect.

The women's liberation movement is difficult to describe, because it is both diverse and diffuse. There is no one central organization, as was characteristic of the first feminist movement; there are no reliable figures for membership, since joining the movement is not a formal act; there is considerable disagreement within the movement itself about leadership, with some feminists disturbed about media-created "superstars" who do not represent the mass of women involved in women's liberation. It is, however, possible to achieve some understanding of the interests and activities of today's feminists through their writings, as this seems to be a highly literate movement which carries on considerable debate through position papers and magazine articles. This section presents five selections, representing different phases of the women's liberation movement, and describing different areas of activism.

Alice S. Rossi's explanation of the post-1920 decline of feminism (Reading 14), and Betty Friedan's prescription to liberate women from the feminine mystique (Reading 15), represent the early stages of the second wave of feminism in this country. In contrast, Marlene Dixon's 1969 article, "Why Women's Liberation?" (Reading 16), represents an early statement of radical feminism, attacking the institution of marriage as oppressive of women, and summarizing some of the history of the radical wing of the women's liberation movement. It is evident from Dixon's argument, as it is from Friedan's more moderate prescription, that the very existence of the women's liberation movement is changing the relations between the sexes, in ways that an earlier generation of feminists only dreamed of achieving. Some illustration of this is provided by "The Politics of Housework," in which Pat Mainardi describes the way in which an apparently trivial issue can be expanded to provide a paradigm of the whole question of sex roles and their characteristics (Reading 17). One of the ways in which women have tried to help each other escape from the stereotyped roles of a sexist society is the consciousness-raising group, described by the editors of *Ms.*, a feminist magazine, in Reading 18.

These selections do not represent the entire women's liberation movement. The movement is not monolithic, and is constantly changing. What these readings can do is illustrate the range and variety of positions and issues characteristic of the second wave of American feminism.

Alice S. Rossi

Why Feminism Declined

*Although Americans in the postwar era often assumed that
feminism had faded from view because women had achieved full
equality with men, a few perceptive observers realized that equality had yet to be attained. One sociologist, Alice S. Rossi, in an
essay provocatively titled "Equality Between the Sexes: An Immodest Proposal," suggested other reasons for the decline of
feminism, and proposed institutional changes to support the
eradication of sex-role stereotypes in order to enable women to
reach full equality. In the following selection, Rossi describes the
decline of feminism, explaining the social and intellectual forces
that led to the feminine mystique.*

WHY FEMINISM DECLINED

I shall discuss three factors which have been major contributors
to the waning of feminism. The chief goals of the early leaders of
the feminist movement were to secure the vote for women and
to change the laws affecting marriage so that women would have

SOURCE: Alice S. Rossi, "Equality Between the Sexes: An Immodest Proposal," in *The Woman in America, Daedalus,* Robert Jay Lifton, Ed., vol.
93, Spring 1964. Reprinted by permission of the American Academy of Arts
and Sciences from *The Woman In America* edited by Robert Jay Lifton.
Copyright © by the American Academy of Arts and Sciences.

equal rights to property and to their own children. As in any social reform movement or social revolution, the focus in the first stage is on change in the legal code, whether this is to declare independence from a mother country, establish a constitution for a new nation, free the slaves, or secure the right of women to be equal citizens with men. But the social changes required to translate such law into the social fabric of a society are of a quite different order. Law by itself cannot achieve this goal. It is one thing to declare slaves free or to espouse a belief in racial equality; quite another matter to accept racial integration in all spheres of life, as many northern communities have learned in recent years. In a similar way, many people accept the legal changes which have reduced the inequality between men and women and espouse belief in sex equality, but resist its manifestation in their personal life. If a social movement rests content with legal changes without making as strong an effort to change the social institutions through which they are expressed, it will remain a hollow victory.

This is one of the things which occurred in the case of the feminist movement. Important as the franchise is, or the recent change in Civil Service regulations which prevents the personnel specification of "male only," the new law or regulation can be successful only to the extent that women exercise the franchise, or are trained to be qualified for and to aspire for the jobs they are now permitted to hold. There is no sex equality until women participate on an equal basis with men in politics, occupations and the family. Law and administrative regulations must permit such participation, but women must want to participate and be able to participate. In politics and the occupational world, to be able to participate depends primarily on whether home responsibilities can be managed simultaneously with work or political commitments. Since women have had, and probably will continue to have, primary responsibility for child-rearing, their participation in politics, professions or the arts cannot be equal to that of men unless ways are devised to ease the combination of home and work responsibilities. This is precisely what has not occurred; at the same time, fewer women today choose a career over marriage, the result has been a reduction in women's representation in the more challenging and demanding occupations.

By itself, the stress on legal change to the neglect of institutional change in the accommodations between family and work does not go very far in explaining why the feminist movement has lost momentum. There is an important second factor which must be viewed in conjunction with this first one. The feminist movement has always been strongest when it was allied with other social reform movements. In the nineteenth century its linkage was with the antislavery movement, and in the early twentieth century it was allied to the social welfare movement. There is an interesting and a simple explanation of this: unlike any other type of social inequality, whether of race, class, religion or nationality, sex is the only instance in which representatives of the unequal groups live in more intimate association with each other than with members of their own group. A woman is more intimately associated with a man than she is with any woman.* This was not the case for lord-serf, master-slave, Protestant-Roman Catholic, white-Negro relationships unless or until the social groups involved reach a full equality. By linking the feminist cause to the antislavery or social welfare movement, women were able to work together with men of similar sympathies and in the process they enlisted the support of these men for the feminist cause. To a greater extent than any other underprivileged group, women need not only vigorous spokesmen and pacesetters of their own sex, but the support of men, to effect any major change in the status of women, whether in the personal sphere of individual relationships or on the level of social organization.† The decline of political radicalism and the gen-

---

* This is one among many points of crucial and still relevant significance to be found in John Stuart Mill's essay "The Subjection of Women" (London, 1869).

† In recent years of acute manpower shortages in scientific, professional and technical fields, there has been a growing awareness of the fact that women constitute the only sizable remaining reservoir of such talent. Many men whose administrative or policy responsibilities alert them to this fact have been eagerly exploring the ways by which female brainpower could be added to the national pool of skilled manpower. The contemporary period is therefore ripe with opportunities for talented women, and women can anticipate a welcome from male colleagues and employers. I shall not discuss any further the current societal need for women in the labor force, because I would argue for an extension of female participation in the higher levels of occupations even in an era with *no* pressing manpower shortages, on the grounds of the more general principles to be developed in this essay.

eral state of affluence and social conservatism in American society since World War II have contributed in subtle ways to the decline of feminism, for women are not joined with men in any movement affecting an underprivileged group in American society. At the present time, marriage remains the only major path of social mobility for women in our society.

The general conservatism of the total society has also penetrated the academic disciplines, with side effects on the motivation and ability of women to exercise the rights already theirs or to press for an extension of them. Feminism has been undermined by the conservatism of psychology and sociology in the postwar period. Sociologists studying the family have borrowed heavily from selective findings in social anthropology and from psychoanalytic theory and have pronounced sex to be a universally necessary basis for role differentiation in the family. By extension, in the larger society women are seen as predominantly fulfilling nurturant, expressive functions and men the instrumental, active functions. When this viewpoint is applied to A.merican society, intellectually aggressive women or tender expressive men are seen as deviants showing signs of "role conflict," "role confusion," or neurotic disturbance. They are not seen as a promising indication of a desirable departure from traditional sex role definitions.* In a similar way, the female sphere, the family, is viewed by social theorists as a passive, pawnlike insti-

---

* Often the conclusion that sex differentiation is a basic and universal phenomenon is buttressed by pointing to a large number of societies, all of which manifest such sex differentiation. Since Americans are easily impressed by large numbers, this does indeed sound like conclusive evidence against the likelihood of any society's achieving full sex equality. Closer examination of such samples, however, reveals two things: very little representation of numerous African societies in which the instrumental-expressive distinction is simply *not* linked to sex in the predicted direction, and second, they are largely primitive societies, a half dozen of which might equal the size of a very small American city. Such cultural comparisons assume every possible kind of societal arrangement is represented, but this is not the case: Sweden, China, Yugoslavia, the Soviet Union, Israel are not represented on such a continuum. I believe we may learn more that is of relevance to a future America by studying family patterns in these societies than from a study of all the primitive societies in the world. Unfortunately, most of contemporary sociology and social anthropology is far less concerned with the future than the present as molded by the past.

tution, adapting to the requirements of the occupational, political or cultural segments of the social structure, seldom playing an active role either in affecting the nature of other social institutions or determining the nature of social change.* The implicit assumption in problem after problem in sociology is that radical social innovations are risky and may have so many unintended consequences as to make it unwise to propose or support them. Although the sociologist describes and analyzes social change, it is change already accomplished, seldom anticipated purposive social change.† When the changes are in process, they are defined as social problems, seldom as social opportunities.

Closely linked to this trend in sociology and social anthropology, and in fact partly attributable to it, is the pervasive permeation of psychoanalytic thinking throughout American society. Individual psychoanalysts vary widely among themselves, but when their theories are popularized by social scientists, marriage and family counselors, writers, social critics, pediatricians and mental health specialists, there emerges a common and conservative image of the woman's role. It is the traditional image of woman which is popularized: the woman who finds complete self-fulfillment in her exclusive devotion to marriage and parenthood. Women who thirty years ago might have chosen a career over a marriage, or restricted their family size to facilitate the combination of family and work roles, have been persuaded to believe that such choices reflect their inadequacy as women. It is this sense of failure as a woman that lies behind the defensive and apologetic note of many older unmarried professional women, the guilt which troubles the working mother (which I suspect

* A rare exception is the recent work by William J. Goode, who has focussed precisely on the active role of the family in determining the course of social change in the non-family segments of social structure. See his *World Revolution and Family Patterns* (Glencoe: The Free Press, 1963).

† When the sociologist finds, for example, that the incidence of divorce is higher for those who marry outside their religion than for those who do not, he concludes that intermarriage is "bad" or "risky"; he does not say such marital failures may reflect the relative newness of the social pattern of intermarriage, much less suggest that such failures may decline once this pattern is more prevalent. In fact, the only aspect of intermarriage which is studied is the incidence of its failure. Sociologists have not studied *successful* intermarriages.

goes up in direct proportion to the degree to which she is familiar with psychoanalytic ideas), the restriction of the level of aspiration of college women, the early plunge into marriage, the closed door of the doll's house.

Our society has been so inundated with psychoanalytic thinking that any dissatisfaction or conflict in personal and family life is considered to require solution on an individual basis. This goes well with the general American value stress on individualism, and American women have increasingly resorted to psychotherapy, the most highly individualized solution of all, for the answers to the problems they have as women. In the process the idea has been lost that many problems, even in the personal family sphere, cannot be solved on an individual basis, but require solution on a societal level by changing the institutional contexts within which we live.

The consequences of this acceptance of psychoanalytic ideas and conservatism in the social sciences have been twofold: first, the social sciences in the United States have contributed very little since the 1930's to any lively intellectual dialogue on sex equality as a goal or the ways of implementing that goal. Second, they have provided a quasi-scientific underpinning to educators, marriage counselors, mass media and advertising researchers, who together have partly created, and certainly reinforced, the withdrawal of millions of young American women from the mainstream of thought and work in our society.*

* A full picture of this post-World War II development is traced in Betty Friedan's *The Feminine Mystique* (New York: W. W. Norton, 1963). See particularly Chapters 6 and 7 on the "Functional Freeze" and the "Sex-Directed Educators."

15   FROM   *Betty Friedan*

A New Life Plan for Women

The second wave of feminism in America emerged in part in reaction to the excesses of the feminine mystique. The retreat into domesticity which had seemed to characterize the female role after the war had not worked well for educated, middle-class women, particularly after their children reached maturity. The widespread popular conviction that women had achieved full equality with men was challenged by the report of a Presidential Commission on the Status of Women, indicating substantial discrimination in salaries and in employment. At the same time, young women in the civil rights and New Left movement, concerned for the rights of others, discovered that they had been relegated to secondary positions in those movements.

Betty Friedan's enormously influential book, The Feminine Mystique, *appeared in this context in 1963. Friedan described, in some detail, the development of the feminine mystique in the postwar period, delineated its insidious effects on women and, in the following selection, proposed a new life plan for women designed to encourage them to abandon the false security of traditional domesticity.*

. . . The problem that has no name—which is simply the fact that American women are kept from growing to their full human capacities—is taking a far greater toll on the physical and mental health of our country than any known disease. Consider the high incidence of emotional breakdown of women in the "role crises" of their twenties and thirties; the alcoholism and suicides in their forties and fifties; the housewives' monopolization of all doctors' time. Consider thè prevalence of teenage marriages, the growing rate of illegitimate pregnancies, and even more seriously, the pathology of mother-child symbiosis. Consider the alarming pas-

SOURCE: Reprinted from *The Feminine Mystique* by Betty Friedan by permission of W. W. Norton Co., Inc. Copyright © 1974, 1963 by Betty Friedan. Also reprinted by permission of Lawrence Pollinger, Ltd.

sivity of American teenagers. If we continue to produce millions of young mothers who stop their growth and education short of identity, without a strong core of human values to pass on to their children, we are committing, quite simply, genocide, starting with the mass burial of American women and ending with the progressive dehumanization of their sons and daughters.

These problems cannot be solved by medicine, or even by psychotherapy. We need a drastic reshaping of the cultural image of femininity that will permit women to reach maturity, identity, completeness of self, without conflict with sexual fulfillment. A massive attempt must be made by educators and parents—and ministers, magazine editors, manipulators, guidance counselors—to stop the early-marriage movement, stop girls from growing up wanting to be "just a housewife," stop it by insisting, with the same attention from childhood on that parents and educators give to boys, that girls develop the resources of self, goals that will permit them to find their own identity.

It is, of course, no easier for an educator to say "no" to the feminine mystique than for an individual girl or woman. Even the most advanced of educators, seriously concerned with the desperate need of housewives with leftover lives on their hands, hesitate to buck the tide of early marriage. They have been brow-beaten by the oracles of popularized psychoanalysis and still tremble with guilt at the thought of interfering with a woman's sexual fulfillment. The rearguard argument offered by the oracles who are, in some cases, right on college campuses themselves, is that since the primary road to identity for a woman is marriage and motherhood, serious educational interests or commitments which may cause conflicts in her role as wife and mother should be postponed until the ·childbearing years are over. . . .

The fact remains that the girl who wastes—as waste she does— her college years without acquiring serious interests, and wastes her early job years marking time until she finds a man, gambles with the possibilities for an identity of her own, as well as the possibilities for sexual fulfillment and wholly affirmed motherhood. The educators who encourage a woman to postpone larger interests until her children are grown make it virtually impossible for her ever to acquire them. It is not that easy for a woman

who has defined herself wholly as wife and mother for ten or
fifteen or twenty years to find new identity at thirty-five or forty
or fifty. The ones who are able to do it are, quite frankly, the
ones who made serious commitments to their earlier education,
the ones who wanted and once worked at careers, the ones who
bring to marriage and motherhood a sense of their own identity
—not those who somehow hope to acquire it later on. A recent
study of fifty women college graduates in an eastern suburb and
city, the year after the oldest child had left home, showed that,
with very few exceptions, the only women who had any interests
to pursue—in work, in community activities, or in the arts—had
acquired them in college. The ones who lacked such interests
were not acquiring them now; they slept late, in their "empty
nests," and looked forward only to death.

Educators at every women's college, at every university, junior
college, and community college, must see to it that women make
a lifetime commitment (call it a "life plan," a "vocation," a "life
purpose" if that dirty word *career* has too many celibate connota-
tions) to a field of thought, to work of serious importance to
society. They must expect the girl as well as the boy to take
some field seriously enough to want to pursue it for life. This
does not mean abandoning liberal education for women in favor
of "how to" vocational courses. Liberal education, as it is given
at the best of colleges and universities, not only trains the mind
but provides an ineradicable core of human values. But liberal
education must be planned for serious use, not merely dilettant-
ism or passive appreciation. As boys at Harvard or Yale or
Columbia or Chicago go on from the liberal arts core to study
architecture, medicine, law, science, girls must be encouraged to
go on, to make a life plan. It has been shown that girls with this
kind of a commitment are less eager to rush into early marriage,
less panicky about finding a man, more responsible for their sexual behavior. Most of them marry, of course, but on a much more
mature basis. Their marriages then are not an escape but a commitment shared by two people that becomes part of their commitment to themselves and society. If, in fact, girls are educated to
make such commitments, the question of sex and when they
marry will lose its overwhelming importance. It is the fact that
women have no identity of their own that makes sex, love, mar-

riage, and children seem the only and essential facts of women's life. . . .

It is essential, above all, for educators themselves to say "no" to the feminine mystique and face the fact that the only point in educating women is to educate them to the limit of their ability. Women do not need courses in "marriage and the family" to marry and raise families; they do not need courses in home-making to make homes. But they must study science—to discover in science; study the thought of the past—to create new thought; study society—to pioneer in society. Educators must also give up these "one thing at a time" compromises. That separate layering of "education," "sex," "marriage," "motherhood," "interests for the last third of life," will not solve the role crisis. Women must be educated to a new integration of roles. The more they are encouraged to make that new life plan—integrating a serious, lifelong commitment to society with marriage and motherhood— the less conflicts and unnecessary frustrations they will feel as wives and mothers, and the less their daughters will make mistaken choices for lack of a full image of woman's identity. . . .

Education itself can help provide that new image—and the spark in girls to create their own—as soon as it stops compromising and temporizing with the old image of "woman's role." For women as well as men, education is and must be the matrix of human evolution. If today American women are finally breaking out of the housewife trap in search of new identity, it is quite simply because so many women have had a taste of higher education—unfinished, unfocused, but still powerful enough to force them on. . . .

Education and re-education of American women for a serious purpose cannot be effected by one or two far-sighted institutions; it must be accomplished on a much wider scale. And no one serves this end who repeats, even for expedience or tact, the clichés of the feminine mystique. It is quite wrong to say, as some of the leading women educators are saying today, that women must of course use their education, but not, heaven forbid, in careers that will compete with men. When women take their education and their abilities seriously and put them to use, ultimately they have to compete with men. It is better for a woman to compete impersonally in society, as men do, than to compete for dominance in her own home with her husband, compete with her neighbors for empty status, and so smother her son that he cannot compete at all. . . .

It also is time to stop giving lip service to the idea that there are no battles left to be fought for women in America, that women's rights have already been won. It is ridiculous to tell girls to keep quiet when they enter a new field, or an old one, so the men will not notice they are there. In almost every professional field, in business and in the arts and sciences, women are still treated as second-class citizens. It would be a great service to tell girls who plan to work in society to expect this subtle, uncomfortable discrimination—tell them not to be quiet, and hope it will go away, but fight it. A girl should not expect special privileges because of her sex, but neither should she "adjust" to prejudice and discrimination.

She must learn to compete then, not as a woman, but as a human being. Not until a great many women move out of the fringes into the mainstream will society itself provide the arrangements for their new life plan. But every girl who manages to stick it out through law school or medical school, who finishes her M.A. or Ph.D. and goes on to use it, helps others move on. Every woman who fights the remaining barriers to full equality which are masked by the feminine mystique makes it easier for the next woman. The very existence of the President's Commission on the Status of Women, under Eleanor Roosevelt's leadership, creates a climate where it is possible to recognize and do something about discrimination against women, in terms not only of pay but of the subtle barriers to opportunity. Even in politics, women must make their contribution not as "housewives" but as citizens. It is, perhaps, a step in the right direction when a woman protests nuclear testing under the banner of "Women Strike for Peace." But why does the professional illustrator who heads the movement say she is "just a housewife," and her followers insist that once the testing stops, they will stay happily at home with their children? Even in the city strongholds of the big political party machines, women can—and are beginning to—change the insidious unwritten rules which let them do the political housework while the men make the decisions.

When enough women make life plans geared to their real abilities, and speak out for maternity leaves or even maternity sabbaticals, professionally run nurseries, and the other changes in the rules that may be necessary, they will not have to sacrifice the right to honorable competition and contribution anymore than they will have to sacrifice marriage and motherhood. It is wrong to keep spelling out unnecessary choices that make women unconsciously resist either commitment or motherhood—and that hold back recognition of the needed social changes. It is not a question of women having their cake and eating it, too. A woman is handicapped by her sex, and handicaps society, either by slavishly copying the pattern of man's advance in the professions, or by refusing to compete with man at all. But with the vision to make a new life plan of her own, she can fulfill a commitment to profession and politics, and to marriage and motherhood with equal seriousness. . . .

In the light of woman's long battle for emancipation, the recent sexual counterrevolution in America has been perhaps a final crisis, a strange breath-holding interval before the larva breaks out of the shell into maturity—a moratorium during which many millions of women put themselves on ice and stopped growing. They say that one day science will be able to make the human body live longer by freezing its growth. American women lately have been living much longer than men— walking through their leftover lives like living dead women. Perhaps men may live longer in America when women carry more of the burden of the battle with the world, instead of being a burden themselves. I think their wasted energy will continue to be destructive to their husbands, to their children, and to themselves until it is used in their own battle with the world. But when women as well as men emerge from biological living to realize their human selves, those leftover halves of life may become their years of greatest fulfillment.

Then the split in the image will be healed, and daughters will not face that jumping-off point at twenty-one or forty-one. When their mothers' fulfillment makes girls sure they want to be women, they will not have to "beat themselves down" to be feminine; they can stretch and stretch until their own efforts will tell them who they are. They will not need the regard of boy or man to feel alive. And when women do not need to live through their husbands and children, men will not fear the love and strength of women, nor need another's weakness to prove their own masculinity. They can finally see each other as they are. And this may be the next step in human evolution. Who knows what women can be when they are finally free to become themselves? Who knows what women's intelligence will contribute when it can be nourished without denying love? Who knows of the possibilities of love when men and women share not only children, home, and garden, not only the fulfillment of their biological roles, but the responsibilities and passions of the work that creates the human future and the full human knowledge of who they are? It has barely begun, the search of women for themselves. But the time is at hand when the voices of the feminine mystique can no longer drown out the inner voice that is driving women on to become complete.

16 FROM   *Marlene Dixon*

Why Women's Liberation—2?

By the end of the 1960s, a widespread and wide-ranging women's liberation movement had developed. Moderate, reformist groups such as the National Organization of Women, organized by Betty Friedan in 1965, emphasized legal action to redress women's grievances. More radical and loosely organized groups grew out of the New Left and antiwar movement, and, in the late sixties, concentrated on organizing women and exploring the psychology of female oppression. Marlene Dixon's article, excerpted in the next selection, represents this radical wing of the women's movement. The selection includes Dixon's critical analysis of the institution of marriage, which is reminiscent of the critiques of Goldman and Gilman.

SOURCE: Copyright © 1972 by Marlene Dixon. Reprinted from *Female Liberation: History and Current Politics*, edited by Roberta Salper, by permission of Alfred A. Knopf, Inc.

... The three major groups that make up the new women's movement—working women, middle-class married women, and students—bring very different kinds of interests and objectives to women's liberation. Working women are most concerned with the economic issues of guaranteed employment, fair wages, job discrimination, and child care. Their most immediate oppression is rooted in industrial capitalism and felt directly through the vicissitudes of an exploitative labor market.

Middle-class women, oppressed by the psychological mutilation and injustice of institutionalized segregation, discrimination, and imposed inferiority, are most sensitive to the dehumanizing consequences of severely limited lives. Usually well educated and capable, these women are rebelling against being forced to trivialize their lives, to live vicariously through husbands and children.

Students, as unmarried, middle-class girls, have been most sensitized to the sexual exploitation of women. They have experienced the frustration of one-way relationships in which the girl is forced into a "wife" and companion role with none of the supposed benefits of marriage. Young women have increasingly rebelled not only against passivity and dependency in their relationships, but also against the notion that they must function as sexual objects, being defined in purely sexual rather than human terms, and being forced to package and sell themselves as commodities on the sex market.

Each group represents an independent aspect of the total institutionalized oppression of women. Yet, in varying degrees all women suffer from economic exploitation, from psychological deprivation, and from exploitive sexuality. Within women's liberation there is a growing understanding that the common oppression of women provides the basis for uniting to form a powerful and radical movement. . . .

MARRIAGE: GENESIS OF WOMEN'S REBELLION

The institution of marriage is the chief vehicle for the perpetuation of the oppression of women; it is through the role of wife that the subjugation of women is maintained. In a very real way the role of wife has been the genesis of women's rebellion throughout history.

Looking at marriage from a detached point of view, one may well ask why anyone gets married, much less women. One answer lies in the economics of women's position, for women are so occupationally limited that drudgery in the home is considered to be infinitely superior to drudgery in the factory. Secondly, women themselves have no independent social status. Indeed, there is no clearer index of the social worth of a woman in this society than the fact that she has none in her own right. A woman is first defined by the man to whom she is attached, but more particularly by the man she marries, and secondly by the children she bears and rears—hence the anxiety over sexual attractiveness, the frantic scramble for boyfriends and husbands. Having obtained and married a man, the race is then on to have children, in order that their attractiveness and accomplishments may add more social worth. In a woman, not having children is seen as an incapacity somewhat akin to impotence in a man.

Beneath all of the pressures of the sexual marketplace and the marital status game, however, there is a far more sinister organization of economic exploitation and psychological mutilation. The housewife role, usually defined in terms of the biological duty of a woman to reproduce and her "innate" suitability for a nurturant and companionship role, is actually crucial to industrial capitalism in an advanced state of technological development. In fact, the housewife (some 44 million women of all classes, ethnic groups, and races) provides, unpaid, absolutely essential services and labor. In turn, her assumption of all household duties makes it possible for the man to spend the majority of his time at his work place.

It is important to understand the social and economic exploitation of the married woman, since the real productivity of her labor is denied by the commonly held assumption that she is dependent on her husband, exchanging her keep for emotional and nurturant services. Household labor, including child care, constitutes a huge amount of socially necessary labor. Nevertheless, in a society based on commodity production, it is not usually considered even as 'real work' since it is outside of trade and the marketplace. In a society in which money determines value, women are a group who work outside the money economy. Their work is not worth money, is therefore valueless, is therefore not even real work. And women themselves, who do this valueless work, can hardly be expected to be worth as much as men, who work for money.

Women are essential to the economy not only as free labor, but also as consumers. The American system of capitalism depends for its survival on the consumption of vast amounts of socially wasteful goods, and a prime target for the unloading of this waste is the housewife. She is the purchasing agent for the family, but beyond that she is eager to buy because her own identity depends on her accomplishments as a consumer and her ability to satisfy the wants of her husband and children. This is not, of course, to say that she has any power in the economy. Although she spends the wealth, she does not own or control it— it simply passes through her hands.

In addition to their role as housewives and consumers, increasing numbers of women are taking outside employment. These women leave the home to join an exploited labor force, only to return at night to assume the double burden of housework on top of wage work—that is, they are forced to work at two full-time jobs. No man is required or expected to take on such a burden. The result: two workers from one household in the labor force with no cutback in essential female functions—three for the price of two, quite a bargain. Regardless of her status in the larger society, within the context of the family, the woman's relationship to the man is one of proletariat to bourgeoisie. One consequence of this class division in the family is to weaken the capacity of oppressed men and women to struggle together against it.

For third-world people within the United States, the oppressive nature of marriage is reflected negatively—for example, motherhood out of wedlock is punished, either through discriminatory welfare legislation or through thinly disguised and genocidal programs of enforced sterilization. This society punishes unmarried women even more than it punishes married women. As a result, many third-world and poor white women want help with their families and need a husband in the home. The destruction of families among poor people, as a result of economic exploitation and social oppression, results in the deprivation of every facet of life for poor women and children. White middle-class women, bound up with the psychological oppression of marriage, have often been blind to the extent of suffering—and the extent of the needs—that the deliberate destruction of the families of the poor has created. Unemployment and pauperization through welfare programs creates very different problems than does the experience of boredom in the suburbs.

In all classes and groups, the institution of marriage nonetheless functions to a greater or lesser degree to oppress women; the unity of women of different classes hinges upon our understanding of that common oppression. The nineteenth-century women's movement refused to deal with marriage and sexuality and chose instead to fight for the vote and to elevate the feminine mystique to a political ideology. That decision retarded the movement for decades. But 1969 is not 1889. For one thing, there now exist alternatives to marriage. The cultural revolution—experimentation with life-styles, communal living, collective child rearing— have all come from the rebellion against dehumanized sexual relationships, against the notion of women as sexual commodities, against the hardship, alienation, and loneliness of American life.

Lessons must be learned from the failures of the earlier movement. The feminine mystique must not be mistaken for politics or legislative reform for winning human rights. Women are now at the bottom of their respective worlds and the basis exists for a common focus of struggle for women in American society. It remains for the movement to understand this, to avoid the mistakes of the past, to respond creatively to the possibilities of the present.

17 FROM

Pat Mainardi
The Politics of Housework

In The Feminine Mystique, *Betty Friedan suggested that middle-class, educated women seek fulfillment through work outside the home. Housework could be handled by either domestic workers or efficient use of time and technological aids on the part of the working woman. Once the women's movement was under way, some women challenged this solution, suggesting that domestic labor should be performed by both husband and wife. Pat Mainardi's essay explores the issue of housework, illustrating some of the problems involved in attempts to reject traditional male and female roles.*

"Though women do not complain of the power of husbands, each complains of her own husband, or of the husbands of her friends. It is the same in all other cases of servitude; at least in the commencement of the emancipatory movement. The serfs did not at first complain of the power of the lords, but only of their tyranny."

—JOHN STUART MILL,
On the Subjection of Women

Liberated women—very different from Women's Liberation! The first signals all kinds of goodies, to warm the hearts (not to mention other parts) of the most radical men. The other signals —HOUSEWORK. The first brings sex without marriage, sex before marriage, cozy housekeeping arrangements ("I'm living with this chick") and the self-content of knowing that you're not the kind of man who wants a doormat instead of a woman. That will come later. After all, who wants that old commodity anymore, the Standard American Housewife, all husband, home and kids. The New Commodity, the Liberated Woman, has sex a lot

SOURCE: Pat Mainardi, "The Politics of Housework." Reprinted by permission of the author.

and has a Career, preferably something that can be fitted in with the household chores—like dancing, pottery, or painting.

On the other hand is Women's Liberation—and housework. What? You say this is all trivial? Wonderful! That's what I thought. It seemed perfectly reasonable. We both had careers, both had to work a couple of days a week to earn enough to live on, so why shouldn't we share the housework? So I suggested it to my mate and he agreed—most men are too hip to turn you down flat. You're right, he said. It's only fair.

Then an interesting thing happened. I can only explain it by stating that we women have been brainwashed more than even we can imagine. Probably too many years of seeing television women in ecstasy over their shiny waxed floors or breaking down over their dirty shirt collars. Men have no such conditioning. They recognize the essential fact of housework right from the very beginning. Which is that it stinks.

Here's my list of dirty chores: buying groceries, carting them home and putting them away; cooking meals and washing dishes and pots; doing the laundry, digging out the place when things get out of control; washing floors. The list could go on but the sheer necessities are bad enough. All of us have to do these things, or get someone else to do them for us. The longer my husband contemplated these chores, the more repulsed he became, and so proceeded the change from the normally sweet considerate Dr. Jekyll into the crafty Mr. Hyde who would stop at nothing to avoid the horrors of—housework. As he felt himself backed into a corner laden with dirty dishes, brooms, mops and reeking garbage, his front teeth grew longer and pointier, his fingernails haggled and his eyes grew wild. Housework trivial? Not on your life! Just try to share the burden.

So ensued a dialogue that's been going on for several years. Here are some of the high points:

• "I don't mind sharing the housework, but I don't do it very well. We should each do the things we're best at." MEANING: Unfortunately I'm no good at things like washing dishes or cooking. What I do best is a little light carpentry, changing light bulbs, moving furniture (how often do *you* move furniture?) ALSO MEANING: Historically the lower classes (black men and us) have had hundreds of years experience doing menial jobs. It would be a waste of manpower to train someone else to do them now. ALSO MEANING: I don't like the dull stupid boring jobs, so you should do them.

• "I don't mind sharing the work, but you'll have to show me how to do it." MEANING: I ask a lot of questions and you'll have to show me everything every time I do it because I don't remember so good. Also don't try to sit down and read while I'M doing my jobs because I'm going to annoy hell out of you until it's easier to do them yourself.

• "We used to be so happy!" (Said whenever it was his turn to do something.) MEANING: I used to be so happy. MEANING: Life without housework is bliss. No quarrel here. Perfect Agreement.

• "We have different standards, and why should I have to work to your standards? That's unfair." MEANING: If I begin to get bugged by the dirt and crap I will say, "This place sure is a sty" or "How can anyone live like this?" and wait for your reaction. I know that all women have a sore called "Guilt over a messy house" or "Household work is ultimately my responsibility." I know that men have caused that sore—if anyone visits and the place *is* a sty, they're not going to leave and say, "He sure is a lousy housekeeper." You'll take the rap in any case. I can outwait you. ALSO MEANING: I can provoke innumerable scenes over the housework issue. Eventually doing all the housework yourself will be less painful to you than trying to get me to do half. Or I'll suggest we get a maid. She will do my share of the work. You will do yours. It's women's work.

• "I've got nothing against sharing the housework, but you can't make me do it on your schedule." MEANING: Passive resistance. I'll do it when I damned well please, if at all. If my job is doing dishes, it's easier to do them once a week. If taking out laundry, once a month. If washing the floors, once a year. If you don't like it, do it yourself oftener, and then I won't do it at all.

• "I hate it more than you. You don't mind it so much." MEANING: Housework is garbage work. It's the worst crap I've ever done. It's degrading and humiliating for someone of *my* intelligence to do it. But for someone of *your* intelligence. . . .

• "Housework is too trivial to even talk about." MEANING: It's even more trivial to do. Housework is beneath my status.

My purpose in life is to deal with matters of significance. Yours is to deal with matters of insignificance. You should do the housework.

• "This problem of housework is not a man–woman problem. In any relationship between two people one is going to have a stronger personality and dominate. MEANING: That stronger personality had better be *me*.

• "In animal societies, wolves, for example, the top animal is usually a male even where he is not chosen for brute strength but on the basis of cunning and intelligence. Isn't that interesting?" MEANING: I have historical, psychological, anthropological and biological justification for keeping you down. How can you ask the top wolf to be equal?

• "Women's Liberation isn't really a political movement." MEANING: The Revolution is coming too close to home. ALSO MEANING: I am only interested in how I am oppressed, not how I oppress others. Therefore the war, the draft and the university are political. Women's Liberation is not.

• "Man's accomplishments have always depended on getting help from other people, mostly women. What great man would have accomplished what he did if he had to do his own housework?" MEANING: Oppression is built into the system and I, as the white American male, receive the benefits of this system. I don't want to give them up.

Participatory democracy begins at home. If you are planning to implement your politics, there are certain things to remember:

1. He *is* feeling it more than you. He's losing some leisure and you're gaining it. The measure of your oppression is his resistance.

2. A great many American men are not accustomed to doing monotonous repetitive work which never issues in any lasting, let alone important, achievement. This is why they would rather repair a cabinet than wash dishes. If human endeavors are like a pyramid with man's highest achievements at the top, then keeping oneself alive is at the bottom. Men have always had servants (us) to take care of this bottom strata of life while they have confined their efforts to the rarefied upper regions. It is thus ironic when they ask of women—where are your great painters,

statesmen, etc. Mme Matisse ran a millinery shop so he could
paint. Mrs. Martin Luther King kept his house and raised his
babies.

3. It is a traumatizing experience for someone who has always
thought of himself as being against any oppression or exploitation of one human being by another to realize that in his daily
life he has been accepting and implementing (and benefiting
from) this exploitation; that his rationalization is little different
from that of the racist who says "Black people don't feel pain"
(women don't mind doing the shitwork); and that the oldest
form of oppression in history has been the oppression of 50%
of the population by the other 50%.

4. Arm yourself with some knowledge of the psychology of
oppressed peoples everywhere, and a few facts about the animal
kingdom. I admit playing top wolf or who runs the gorillas is
silly but as a last resort men bring it up all the time. Talk about
bees. If you feel really hostile bring up the sex life of spiders.
They have sex. She bites off his head.

The psychology of oppressed peoples is not silly. Jews, immigrants, black men and all women have employed the same psychological mechanisms to survive: admiring the oppressor,
glorifying the oppressor, wanting to be like the oppressor, wanting the oppressor to like them, mostly because the oppressor held
all the power.

5. In a sense, all men everywhere are slightly schizoid—
divorced from the reality of maintaining life. This makes it
easier for them to play games with it. It is almost a cliché that
women feel greater grief at sending a son off to a war or losing
him to that war because they bore him, suckled him, and raised
him. The men who foment those wars did none of those things
and have a more superficial estimate of the worth of human life.
One hour a day is a low estimate of the amount of time one has
to spend "keeping" oneself. By foisting this off on others, man has
seven hours a week—one working day more to play with his mind
and not his human needs. Over the course of generations it is
easy to see whence evolved the horrifying abstractions of modern
life.

6. With the death of each form of oppression, life changes and
new forms evolve. English aristocrats at the turn of the century

were horrified at the idea of enfranchising workingmen—were sure that it signalled the death of civilization and a return to barbarism. Some workingmen were even deceived by this line. Similarly with the minimum wage, abolition of slavery, and female suffrage. Life changes but it goes on. Don't fall for any line about the death of everything if men take a turn at the dishes. They will imply that you are holding back the Revolution (their Revolution). But you are advancing it (your Revolution).

7. Keep checking up. Periodically consider who's actually *doing* the jobs. These things have a way of backsliding so that a year later once again the woman is doing everything. After a year make a list of jobs the man has rarely if ever done. You will find cleaning pots, toilets, refrigerators and ovens high on the list. Use time sheets if necessary. He will accuse you of being petty. He is above that sort of thing (housework). Bear in mind what the worst jobs are, namely the ones that have to be done every day or several times a day. Also the ones that are dirty—it's more pleasant to pick up books, newspapers, etc., than to wash dishes. Alternate the bad jobs. It's the daily grind that gets you down. Also make sure that you don't have the responsibility for the housework with occasional help from him. "I'll cook dinner for you tonight" implies it's really your job and isn't he a nice guy to do some of it for you.

8. Most men had a rich and rewarding bachelor life during which they did not starve or become encrusted with crud or buried under the litter. There is a taboo that says women mustn't strain themselves in the presence of men—we haul around 50 lbs of groceries if we have to but aren't allowed to open a jar if there is someone around to do it for us. The reverse side of the coin is that men aren't supposed to be able to take care of themselves without a woman. Both are excuses for making women do the housework.

9. Beware of the double whammy. He won't do the little things he always did because you're now a "Liberated Woman," right? Of course he won't do anything else either. . . .

I was just finishing this when my husband came in and asked what I was doing. Writing a paper on housework. Housework?

he said, *Housework?* Oh my god how trivial can you get. A paper on housework.

LITTLE POLITICS OF HOUSEWORK QUIZ

1. The lowest job in the army, used as punishment is *(a) working 9–5 (b) kitchen duty (K.P).*
2. When a man lives with his family, his *(a) father (b) mother* does his housework.
3. When he lives with a woman, *(a) he (b) she* does the housework.
4. *(a) His son (b) His daughter* learns in preschool how much fun it is to iron daddy's handkerchief.
5. From the New York *Times,* 9/21/69: "Former Greek Official George Mylonas pays the penalty for differing with the ruling junta in Athens by performing household chores on the island of Amorgos where he lives in forced exile" (with hilarious photo of a miserable Mylonas carrying his own water). What the *Times* means is that he ought to have *(a) indoor plumbing (b) a maid.*
6. Dr. Spock said *(Redbook,* 3/69) "Biologically and temperamentally I believe, women were made to be concerned first and foremost with child care, husband care, and home care." Think about *(a) who made us (b) why? (c) what is the effect on their lives (d) what is the effect on our lives?*
7. From *Time,* 1/5/70, "Like their American counterparts, many housing project housewives are said to suffer from neurosis. And for the first time in Japanese history, many young husbands today complain of being henpecked. Their wives are beginning to demand detailed explanations when they don't come home straight from work and some Japanese males nowadays are even compelled to do housework." According to *Time,* women become neurotic *(a) when they are forced to do the maintenance work for the male caste all day every day of their lives* or *(b) when they no longer want to do the maintenance work for the male caste all day every day of their lives.*

Consciousness-Raising

The women's liberation movement has been characterized by an emphasis on organizing women to perceive their own oppression and take steps to free themselves, as well as by more traditional efforts to change laws and social patterns to facilitate this liberation. One technique, consciousness-raising, has been widely used by women's groups to encourage participants to explore their own perceptions of themselves and the ways in which they have been repressed and restricted. The following description of a consciousness-raising group was designed to serve new groups as a guide and provides insight into some of the internal processes of the current women's movement.

Freedom is a very contagious idea. All over the country, women have caught the bug, understood very clearly what is wrong with their lives, and begun to ask the hard questions:

"How do I stop playing the same old role every day?"

"How do I change my husband? my boss? my family? my friends? the limitations that surround me?"

And, hardest of all, "How do I change myself?"

Many have begun to find the answers for themselves and for other women in the intimate and supportive talk sessions known as consciousness-raising or rap groups. Without the traditions of psychiatry or encounter-group therapy, which so often assumed that mental health meant playing the classical male-female roles, these gatherings are free to search out new solutions, new identities, and new techniques. They are the heart and soul of the Women's Movement.

SOURCE: "A Guide to Consciousness-Raising," reprinted with permission from *Ms.* Magazine, July 1972.

WHY?

Women have been isolated from each other. In our kitchens and even in our outside jobs, we are often made to feel that our problems are ours and ours alone; that somehow everything stifling and painful about our lives is due to our personal inadequacies; that, if there weren't something wrong with us in the first place, we would be perfectly happy and fulfilled in the female role.

Men have problems, too, of course, even in their less limited worlds; but theirs are somewhat adult and legitimate, and therefore can be discussed over a business lunch or dignified by sympathy at home. Even minority men have someplace they can be themselves—a part of town, a bar, some turf that belongs to them—but women of every group have almost no place where roles as wife, mother, sex object, hostess, high-level helper, social appendage, or domestic aren't forced upon us.

The result is that we don't know who we are; we can't separate our individual selves from our social conditioning. Worse, we feel guilty or self-indulgent or crazy for wanting such a separation.

The rap group is a free place; a place to be honest. It is a group of supportive and nonjudging friends who are there to help when we come back battered or ridiculed from trying to change our worlds. It is some version of the often repeated statement, "*You* feel like that? My God, I thought only *I* felt like that." It is a place to discover and sustain each other and ourselves.

Eventually, we find our not only who we are, but the political relationship of women, as a caste, to society as a whole. We learn or invent practical ways of changing our own lives, and the lives of women around us.

WHO?

It is important that the group be totally women. Husbands and male friends or co-workers may resent this at first, but their presence makes it much harder for us to speak honestly, and to venture out from under our habitual roles and patterns. Even well-meaning men tend to adopt an attitude of helpful paternalism, and less enlightened ones take over the focus of a group by becoming adversaries—symbolic enemies to be defeated or convinced. Women need to be by themselves. Men who really want to be helpful will care for houses and children so that women may be free to take part, or they will start rap groups of their own, to discuss the ways they are restricted by their "masculine" role.

Rap groups can start anywhere, but most often they happen among friends, neighbors, co-workers, or classmates. This may make for a homogeneous group where age and social background are similar. Others start at large meetings of women, who—realizing their need for longer, deeper contact—form smaller groups. Still other groups are strangers who are put together by a local Women's Center. Groups that are not homogeneous take longer to break through differences of style, but have the advantage of showing dramatically how women's problems tend to survive the boundaries of age, economic status, and ethnic background.

The important requirement for a rap group is that the members be serious about their desire for life changes, and that they resepct that need in each other. Given the intimacy and willingness to make ourselves vulnerable that are necessary for consciousness-raising, trust in confidentiality is essential, especially when members know each other in outside contexts.

The optimum size is six to ten women; larger groups make individual participation difficult. Since all the members may not find the group personally right, however, and since there may be dropouts for other reasons, it's safe to start with as many as fifteen.

Adding new members after, say, the second or third session is not a good idea. Coming in without knowledge of what's gone before is hard on the newcomer, and hard on the group.

WHERE?

Most groups take turns meeting at each other's homes, if such rotation is practical. Giving shelter to the group, seeing it function in rooms we live with intimately, is part of the process. If some members feel ashamed (or inordinately proud) of where they live, that should not stand in the way, but can become a good topic for group discussion.

Privacy is still the most important requirement, however, and some women will have husbands, children, men friends, or roommates who will make this impossible. Those members may exempt themselves from the turn-taking, or the whole group may choose some neutral place to meet.

Transportation and food should be managed so no one is excluded for financial reasons. Many groups ask each individual to bring along her own food, or some item to contribute to a communal meal, so that no member is made to play hostess, with all the social habits that role implies.

The group should also share babysitting expenses of its members in whatever way is practical, with women who don't have children contributing, too, in order to help women who do.

WHEN?

Most groups find one meeting a week maintains intimacy, without causing too much hardship. In the early, exhilarating stages, however, or in times of crisis for one or more members, the group may choose to meet more often.

Evening meetings allow for open-ended sessions, but daytime may be better for women who are at home. Two to four hours seems to be the average time necessary for everyone to have a chance to take part, but each group must discover its own best time.

Regular attendance is important. Each meeting is a step in a growth process, and each member plays an organic part. Members who are often absent, or come very late, slow down the process. They also may create bad feelings by implying through their actions that the group isn't very important to their lives.

Due to school or family patterns, some groups find it necessary to stop temporarily during the summer. Fall or winter may be the best time to start. The average life of a group seems to be six months to two years. There are no rules, but a substantial duration of time is necessary for substantial growth.

Some groups disband as members become more involved in outside action projects. Others change form, taking on a more activist structure themselves. Still others remain alive as sources of support, refueling, and personal feedback for women who are very active elsewhere.

HOW?

There should be no leader. The consciousness-raising group is specifically designed to eliminate preexisting habits of passivity, dominance, the need for outside instruction, or a hierarchy, even if it is to take care of functional details. If one or several members of the group dominate to a degree that keeps others from participating fully, it is the responsibility of each member to try to set the balance straight. It's often helpful to go around in a circle, starting with a different member at each meeting.

In the beginning, as a temporary tactic, some groups give each member ten tokens, and require that a token be given up each time that individual speaks. The score at the session's end helps us to realize who is listening too much, and who is not listening enough.

It's important that we speak personally, subjectively, and specifically. Generalizing, theorizing, or talking in abstractions is bound to misrepresent or alienate some member of the group to whom those generalizations don't apply.

This personal mode of speaking is called "giving testimony," a phrase that may sound legalistic or religious at first, but has come to describe the first-person rule that is the heart of consciousness-raising.

Do not interrupt while another woman is giving testimony. She should be questioned only for clarification. ("How old were you when that happened?" "What was your reason at the time?") This is perhaps the greatest advantage consciousness-raising has over open discussion. With the assurance of an attentive audience for a specified length of time, a woman is relieved of the pressure of trying to make herself heard over others, or waiting anxiously for the right moment to speak. She is able to pause, to think something through. The rest of the group is also free to listen instead of waiting for a chance to seize the platform. The result is that things are said that might never otherwise emerge in group discussion. The emotional range of the group is extended to include quieter, more intimate feelings which could previously only be shared in one-to-one situations. For many women, it is the first time they have ever been listened to seriously by a group.

Don't give advice, or judge a woman's testimony. After each woman has spoken, there can be time for questions and elaboration, but an attempt to question her facts or offer a personal solution is rarely called for. In describing personal feelings and experience, there is no right or wrong.

This rule of never challenging another woman's experience may be the hardest one to stick to, but it is also one of the most important. What a sister says may seem inaccurate to you, but it is true for her at that moment. If it is wrong, she must come to realize it herself, not be forced into a defensive position. Keep in mind that she may never have had a chance to talk about herself without being interrupted or challenged by a father, mother, husband, or psychiatrist. Ask yourself why you feel compelled to challenge her. And remember, when it is your turn to speak, no one will challenge you.

Deciding what to talk about may emerge naturally out of the group, but it's important not to spend too much time—especially in the beginning—on daily functional problems. Those are the symptoms, not the disease. On the other hand, plunging into heavy topics, such as sex or marriage, in an early session may make some women feel threatened or defensive. After all, at this stage, the women are still relative strangers.

Most groups find that starting at the beginning works best: childhood and feelings about self and parents raise fewer problems of guilt and defensiveness, since we were less responsible for our lives in those years. Move slowly on from topic to topic, and try to keep a common focus. For instance, a group might explore questions like these:

• What was our earliest childhood awareness of being trained to behave like a girl? How were brothers or boys in the neighborhood raised, treated, or educated differently? What was our feeling about that?

• What was our first experience of sexual fantasies? Sexual realities?

• What was our reaction to bodily changes in adolescence? How were we prepared for those changes? How did we feel?

• What were our earliest fantasies of accomplishment? Of making some difference in the world?

• What was our first work experience? Current work experiences?

• What thoughts are brought to mind by the word, "humiliation"?

• What are our feelings about money? for women? for men?

• What are our feelings about power? when women use it? when men use it?

• Marriage: why did we marry, if we did; why not, if not? Would we make the same choice again?

• How often are we able to be honest about our feelings?

• What situations make us feel guilty?

• How do we feel about our appearance? about wearing makeup, fashionable clothes?

• What are our private terrors?

• How do we feel about childbirth? aging? menopause?

• How do we feel about love? When have our feelings been experienced as love? What are our fears of being unlovable?

• How have our experiences with discrimination against women, whatever their race, compared with experiences of discrimination against black men? Other minorities? What feelings of inferiority have we been taught that are the same? or different?

• What are our hopes for the future? What do we want to do before we die?

• What conditions of our daily lives do we want to change? How are we (or why are we not) changing them?

After each woman has given her testimony, the whole group should discuss the common elements in our experiences, and how that commonality relates to the role of women as a group. Additional thoughts that occurred to women while listening can be discussed, and so can interpersonal problems or discomfort with style. (Language is a key, and can be questioned, too. Why do some of us refer to ourselves as "girls"? What feelings are associated with that? Why are some adjectives used for women and some for men?) The end of each session is a summing up— a time of insight and of sharing books or outside sources that have helped us and might help others.

After the group has grown and changed together, the individual will have grown and changed, too. We will never be quite the same again.

And neither will the world.

PART FIVE

Visions of the Future

Those who attack the status quo are frequently asked how they propose to replace it. Some of the radicals of the New Left grew weary of such questions and refused to be distracted from their struggle for change by attempting to describe the society they were trying to create. Although such questions can divert the energies of radicals and reformers into the creation of airy, and harmless, utopias, they are not invalid. We can learn a great deal about the new feminism by exploring its goals, and by understanding the ways in which those goals are to be achieved. This section thus includes three visions of the future planned by feminists, including both positive and negative aspects, major and minor changes.

Those who comprehend the diversity of the women's liberation movement will not expect one coherent vision of the future to emerge from it. The three women in this section do not agree on the future they foresee. Alice Rossi, writing at the very beginning of the second wave of feminism, sees a new and freer woman emerging from a nonsexist society (Reading 19). In contrast, Caroline Bird, writing in the movement's midstream, argues that the abolition of sex-role stereotypes will be a painful and difficult business, with mixed results (Reading 20). Finally, Shulamith Firestone, a radical feminist, proposes a cybernetic utopia characterized by drastic changes in the family, the economy, in the way we lead our lives, in order to liberate women.

Whatever direction the movement takes, our future will be shaped in some way by the struggle of American women to

119

change their place in society. This generation of feminists is aware of the difficulties that ended the first wave of feminism. We may hope that history will not repeat itself because of that awareness.

19   FROM   *Alice S. Rossi*

                                        Profile

One view of the future of feminism has been provided by Alice S. Rossi, in the conclusion to her essay, "Equality Between the Sexes: An Immodest Proposal," excerpted in Part Four. In the following selection, Rossi describes the development of what might be called the "post-feminist woman," whose life-choices have not been restricted by sexual stereotypes.

In the course of this essay I have suggested a number of institutional innovations in education, residence and child care which would facilitate equality between the sexes. Instead of a more conventional kind of summary, I shall describe a hypothetical case of a woman who is reared and lives out her life under the changed social conditions proposed in this essay.

She will be reared, as her brother will be reared, with a combination of loving warmth, firm discipline, household responsibility and encouragement of independence and self-reliance. She will not be pampered and indulged, subtly taught to achieve her

SOURCE: Alice S. Rossi, "Equality Between the Sexes: An Immodest Proposal," in *The Woman in America, Daedulus,* Robert Jay Lifton, Ed., vol. 93, Spring 1964. Reprinted by permission of the American Academy of Arts and Sciences from *The Woman In America* edited by Robert Jay Lifton. Copyright © by the American Academy of Arts and Sciences.

ends through coquetry and tears, as so many girls are taught today. She will view domestic skills as useful tools to acquire, some of which, like fine cooking or needlework, having their own intrinsic pleasures but most of which are necessary repetitive work best gotten done as quickly and efficiently as possible. She will be able to handle minor mechanical breakdowns in the home as well as her brother can, and he will be able to tend a child, press, sew, and cook with the same easy skills and comfortable feeling his sister has.

During their school years, both sister and brother will increasingly assume responsibility for their own decisions, freely experiment with numerous possible fields of study, gradually narrowing to a choice that best suits their interests and abilities rather than what is considered appropriate or prestigeful work for men and women. They will be encouraged by parents and teachers alike to think ahead to a whole life span, viewing marriage and parenthood as one strand among many which will constitute their lives. The girl will not feel the pressure to belittle her accomplishments, lower her aspirations, learn to be a receptive listener in her relations with boys, but will be as true to her growing sense of self as her brother and male friends are. She will not marry before her adolescence and schooling are completed, but will be willing and able to view the college years as a "moratorium" from deeply intense cross-sex commitments, a period of life during which her identity can be "at large and open and various." Her intellectual aggressiveness as well as her brother's tender sentiments will be welcomed and accepted as *human* characteristics, without the self-questioning doubt of latent homosexuality that troubles many college-age men and women in our era when these qualities are sex-linked.* She will not cling to her parents, nor they to her, but will establish an increasingly larger sphere of her own independent world in which she moves and works, loves and thinks, as a maturing young person. She will learn to take pleasure in her own body

---

* David Riesman has observed that this latent fear of homosexuality haunts the Ivy League campuses, putting pressure on many young men to be guarded in their relations with each other and with their male teachers, reflecting in part the lag in the cultural image of appropriate sex characteristics. See David Riesman, "Permissiveness and Sex Roles," *Marriage and Family Living,* 21 (August, 1959), 211-217.

and a man's body and to view sex as a good and wonderful
experience, but not as an exclusive basis for an ultimate commitment to another person, and not as a test of her competence
as a female or her partner's competence as a male. Because she
will have a many-faceted conception of her self and its worth,
she will be free to merge and lose herself in the sex act with a
lover or a husband.*

* It goes beyond the intended scope of this essay to discuss the effects of a
social pattern of equality between men and women upon their sexual relationship. A few words are, however, necessary, since the defenders of traditional
sex roles often claim that full equality would so feminize men and masculin-
ize women that satisfactory sexual adjustments would be impossible and
homosexuality would probably increase. If the view of the sex act presup-
poses a dominant male actor and a passive female subject, then it is indeed
the case that full sex equality would probably be the death knell of this traditional sexual relationship. Men and women who participate as equals in
their parental and occupational and social roles will complement each other
sexually in the same way, as essentially equal partners, and not as an ascend-
ant male and a submissive female. This does not mean, however, that equality
in non-sexual roles necessarily de-eroticizes the sexual one. The enlarged base
of shared experience can, if anything, heighten the salience of sex *qua* sex.
In Sweden, where men and women approach equality more than perhaps any
other western society, visitors are struck by the erotic atmosphere of that
society. Sexually men and women do after all each lack what the other has
and wishes for completion of the self; the salience of sex may be enhanced
precisely in the situation of the diminished significance of sex as a differen-
tiating factor in all other areas of life. It has always seemed paradoxical to
me that so many psychoanalysts defend the traditional sex roles and warn
that drastic warping of the sexual impulses may flow from full sex equality;
surely they are underestimating the power and force of the very drive which
is in so central a position in their theoretical framework. Maslow is one of
the few psychologists who has explored the connections between sex experience and the conception of self among women. With a sample of one hundred
and thirty college-educated women in their twenties, he found, contrary to
traditional notions of femininity and psychoanalytic theories, that the more
"dominant" the woman, the greater her enjoyment of sexuality, the greater
her ability to give herself freely in love. Women with dominance feelings
were free to be completely themselves, and this was crucial for their full
expression in sex. They were not feminine in the traditional sense, but
enjoyed sexual fulfillment to a much greater degree than the conventionally
feminine women he studied. See A. H. Maslow, "Dominance, Personality and
Social Behavior in Women," *Journal of Social Psychology*, 10 (1939), 3–39;
and "Self-Esteem (Dominance Feeling) and Sexuality in Women," *Journal of
Social Psychology*, 16 (1942), 259–294; or a review of Maslow's studies in
Betty Friedan, *The Feminine Mystique*, pp. 316–326.

Marriage for our hypothetical woman will not mark a withdrawal from the life and work pattern that she has established, just as there will be no sharp discontinuity between her early childhood and youthful adult years. Marriage will be an enlargement of her life experiences, the addition of a new dimension to an already established pattern, rather than an abrupt withdrawal to the home and a turning in upon the marital relationship. Marriage will be a "looking outward in the same direction" for both the woman and her husband. She will marry and bear children only if she deeply desires a mate and children, and will not be judged a failure as a person if she decides against either. She will have few children if she does have them, and will view her pregnancies, childbirth and early months of motherhood as one among many equally important highlights in her life, experienced intensely and with joy but not as the exclusive basis for a sense of self-fulfillment and purpose in life. With planning and foresight, her early years of child bearing and rearing can fit a long-range view of all sides of herself. If her children are not to suffer from "paternal deprivation," her husband will also anticipate that the assumption of parenthood will involve a weeding out of nonessential activities either in work, civic or social participation. Both the woman and the man will feel that unless a man can make room in his life for parenthood, he should not become a father. The woman will make sure, even if she remains at home during her child's infancy, that he has ample experience of being with and cared for by other adults besides herself, so that her return to a full-time position in her field will not constitute a drastic change in the life of the child, but a gradual pattern of increasing supplementation by others of the mother. The children will have a less intense involvement with their mother, and she with them, and they will all be the better for it. When they are grown and establish adult lives of their own, our woman will face no retirement twenty years before her husband, for her own independent activities will continue and expand. She will be neither an embittered wife, an interfering mother-in-law nor an idle parasite, but together with her husband she will be able to live an independent, purposeful and satisfying third act in life.

20 FROM   *Caroline Bird*

                   The Case for Equality

*In the final chapter of her 1969 study of the effects of sex dis-
crimination, Caroline Bird carefully examined the arguments for
equal rights for women. After exploring some of the possible
social benefits of equal rights, Bird, in the following selection,
analyzes the several problems a society committed to sex equality
would face, concluding that despite the possible disadvantages,
equity demanded absolutely equal opportunity for men and
women.*

All this sounds fine, but do women really want it? Doesn't
this radical reallocation of responsibilities overemphasize work?
Won't the world of the future have to cope with leisure rather
than stimulate achievement? Don't we need the special talents
of women to reform business and public life, and won't we lose
their special gifts if we bring them up to be exactly like men?
And finally, won't there be more family quarrels and ground for
conflict when men and women do exactly the same things? And
what about chivalry? Doesn't the financial support men give to
women catalyze something in their relationship that is valuable?

The objections are formidable. The most thoughtful idealists
of 1968 often defend the contribution of womanliness on esthetic
and even spiritual grounds.

"The future of mankind may well depend on the fate of a
'mother variable' uncontrolled by technological man," Erik Erikson, lecturer in psychiatry at Harvard writes. Like many sensitive
people appalled at the mechanical, crowded, impersonal society
we are building, Erikson hopes that the compassion and humanity of women can save us. Idealists who look to women for sal-
vation are often less interested in man-woman relations than in

using women as a natural resource against the collapse of human
values under the impact of technological advance. This is, of
course, a New Masculinist attitude.

The most fervent of these idealistic New Masculinists are men.
In 1964, Vermont Royster, the chief editor of the business-
oriented *Wall Street Journal*, attacked the "Work Mystique"
which in his opinion was misleading women into equating self-
fulfillment with employment. Work is not all that important, he
insisted. In 1967, a *Reader's Digest* editor, Charles W. Ferguson,
articulated this New Masculinist appeal in his book, *The Male
Attitude*, which blamed the parlous state of the world squarely
on stag rule and urged society to save itself, before it was too
late, by making greater use of the neglected insights of women.

What these people are saying is that women are better than
men because they are less tainted with power. They have revived
the Victorian notion of the pure woman, the madonna redeeming
an evil world. The trouble with this flattering assumption is that
women are no purer than they ever were and the history of their
behind-the-scenes or from-the-side influence is as uneventful as
their impact on politics. Women are uncommitted and unorgan-
ized and hence a tempting target for politicians and reformers,
but they have, so far, resisted all attempts to make themselves
better than men. Today's women can't pioneer leisure styles of
living for men any more than yesterday's women could appreci-
ate art and music for men. There is no male side or female side
to the war in Vietnam. A father's son dies for every mother's son
who dies.

With us still are the Old Masculinists who argue that real
equality would leave women worse off than before. And it's true.
Laws that classify by sex are largely designed to protect women
from desertion. They date from the days when marriage, with its
consequent exposure to child-bearing, was the only way a woman
could earn a decent living. But family-support laws are becoming dead letters, and in any case they bear more heavily on the
rich who own property than on the poor who don't have assets
worth attaching. Desertion is the poor man's divorce.

More serious is the possibility that real desegregation would
develop conflicts of interests between husbands and wives that
now occur only rarely. In 1962, the London Stock Exchange

turned down the application of Elisabeth Rivers-Bulkeley for membership because her husband, a Lloyd's insurance broker, was "at business in risk" and she might have a "moral obligation" to meet his debts. But such problems can be solved. If Carolyn Agger, the Washington lawyer, had a case that went to the Supreme Court of the United States, her husband Justice Fortas might elect not to hear the case, or she might get another lawyer to argue it.

A more serious problem for two-income families is our increasing mobility. Salaried workers are frequently moved by their organizations or offered better jobs elsewhere. In Asiatic cultures, separation of the husband and wife for periods is not regarded as serious. Family ties are not personal but legal. In our American upper classes, as in others, husbands and wives often go on separate trips and do not feel that they must be together all the time in every phase of their marriage.

But in a society where men and women are treated equally a wife would not be forced to follow a husband if he were better able to make the sacrifice of location than she, and the move made sense for the partnership, as well. In some cases, key men have refused to move to a new place unless suitable jobs could be found for their wives. Employers could do more of the accommodating than it occurs to them to do now. Federal and state services might lead the way by adopting a policy that the spouse of a transferred worker be given priority on appropriate job openings in the new area; that husbands and wives employed by the service be transferred, insofar as possible, together; and that refusal to move because of employment of a husband or wife may not be held against a civil servant in considering him for promotion.

Finally, there is no avoiding the fact that there are drawbacks. If boys and girls are not to form their characters around the need to be "manly" and "womanly," they will need other models, other motivations. It is realistic to urge a boy to do a dull job because it will benefit him in the future, but it is easier to get him to "act like a man." And because of its visibility, sex difference is a handy way to decide small matters, such as who gets named first in a social introduction. The brave new world of sex equality would be a world of frequent divorce. Divorces increase in good times and decline in bad times, suggesting that many more couples would like to separate than are financially able to. Regardless of cause or effect, the marriages of career women are less stable than the marriages of women financially dependent on their husbands.

Vanguard couples have taken turns working and going to school, but all pioneering requires thought and planning which tradition and habit settle with less effort. The answer is easier to find when the answer is the same for all; if grandmother's marriage seemed calmer, it may have been only that it required fewer personal decisions and women had to make more accommodations. The colleague marriage may be "better" if it comes off, but it takes more energy. It's risky, and it fails noisily.

Parallel to the dangers of choice in family roles are the uncertainties of choice in vocation. When asked why they marry, men often answer "to have something to work for." When asked what they would do if they had enough money to live without working, they say they would continue to work. In the Old Masculinist morality, women symbolize the goal. When a man has a woman to work for, he doesn't have to think any further. Without her, he has to examine his real feelings and motivations.

American women are already confused by the choices they now have of work and home and various combinations of each. Are we to impose this kind of choice on men, too? There is evidence that the intrinsic interest of the work is more important to girls choosing professions than the money they can earn. If boys as well as girls were free to choose work that interested them, we might have a hard time getting dull jobs done. What if everybody wanted to act in television, an occupation which need not increase proportionately to population, while fewer and fewer wanted to become nurses and teachers, occupations which parallel population growth?

The real argument for equality cannot be made on the basis of expedience. The compelling reason is equity. The little jokes the New Masculinists love to make about the New Feminists imply that the difference between the sexes is so beautiful, so rewarding, so deeply rooted, so innocent, and so much fun that it is worth enhancing at the expense of considerable inequity.

Yet equity is not to be dismissed so lightly. It is the sort of blessing that doesn't count when you have it, but ruins everything if you don't. Most Americans are now aware of the enormous social, psychic, and economic cost of Negro slavery. These costs became widely apparent only when the inequity of slavery aroused indignation and set people thinking.

Billions of words and hours of thought have been expanded on the complexities of race relations. Progress, said the sophisticated, will have to be slow. You cannot change a way of life overnight. Yet today it is clear that however agonizing the changes have been, the problem has never been all that complicated. What we did to the Negroes was just plain wrong, and everybody knew it.

So with the employment of women. Relations between the sexes are complicated, and change is hard, but the way women are treated is just plain wrong.

It is wrong to make aspiring women prove they are twice as good as men.

It is wrong to pay women less than men for the same work just because they will work for less.

It is wrong to exclude women from work they can do so that they have to work for less in the jobs open to them.

It is wrong to make aspiring women pay the penalty of women who are content to be used as a labor reserve.

It is wrong to assume that because some women can't do mathematics, *this* woman can't do mathematics.

It is wrong to expect women to work for their families or the nation and then to step aside when their families or the nation want them out of the way.

It is wrong to deny individuals born female the right to inconvenience their families to pursue art, science, power, prestige, money, or even self-expression, in the way that men in pursuit of these goals inconvenience their families as a matter of course.

It is wrong to impute motives to women instead of letting them speak for themselves.

It is wrong to ridicule, sneer, frighten, or brainwash anyone unable to fight back.

It is wrong, as well as wasteful and dangerous, to discourage talent.

All these things are wrong, and everybody knows it. And just as "separate but equal" schools limited white children as well as Negroes, so the doctrine that women are different but equal limits men. Mary Wollstonecraft, John Stuart Mill, George Bernard Shaw, and President Goheen of Princeton were all concerned, and some of them primarily with the damage inequity does to men. David Riesman points out that every boundary we impose on women we impose on men also.

Equity speaks softly and wins in the end. But it is expedience, with its loud voice, that sets the time of victory. The cotton gin did not make slavery wrong, but it helped a lot of Southerners to *see* that slavery was wrong. The immigrant vote did not make woman suffrage right, but it frightened politicians into enfranchising women on the theory that the educated women of politically conservative old American stock would vote more readily than the submissive women of politically unpredictable ethnic groups.

So with equal opportunity for women. Conditions conspire to help people see the inequity and the advantages of ending it. First the pill gives women control over their fate so that they can be as responsible as men. Then modern medicine prolongs the lives of women so that all now have decades of potential working life, beyond child-rearing age, during which none of the limitations imposed on women make sense. Next, modern technology takes their work out of the home and invites them to do it elsewhere, and for pay. It frees more mothers of the work of bringing up children, and gives it to schools. Meanwhile, the new technology is less and less a respecter of old-fashioned sex differences. It eliminated the need for physical strength very rapidly and is now eliminating the need for "detail work."

What the new technology needs is educated manpower that can learn new skills. What it doesn't need is more ordinary people without skills. Both needs strengthen the case for equal opportunity for the underprivileged majority of Americans who were born female.

21 FROM Shulamith Firestone
Alternatives

A considerably more radical view of the possible effects of the women's liberation movement was provided by Shulamith Firestone in 1971. Firestone makes a case for a feminist revolution, to result in what she calls a "cybernetic socialism" as a context for human liberation. In the following selection, Firestone describes a household system designed to replace the nuclear family with a highly flexible program designed to provide the maximum degree of freedom and self-control to all participants, women, men, and children.

HOUSEHOLDS

I shall now outline a system that I believe will satisfy any remaining needs for children after ego concerns are no longer part of our motivations. Suppose a person or a couple at some point in their lives desires to live around children in a family-size unit. While we will no longer have reproduction as the life goal of the normal individual—we have seen how single and group nonreproductive life styles could be enlarged to become satisfactory for many people for their whole lifetimes and for others, for good portions of their lifetime—certain people may still prefer community-style group living permanently, and other people may want to experience it at some time in their lives, especially during early childhood.

Thus at any given time a proportion of the population will want to live in reproductive social structures. Correspondingly, the society in general will still need reproduction, though reduced, if only to create a new generation.

The proportion of the population will be automatically a

SOURCE: Adapted by permission of William Morrow & Company, Inc., from *The Dialectic of Sex* by Shulamith Firestone. Copyright 1970 by Shulamith Firestone. Reprinted also by permission of Laurence Pollinger Limited.

select group with a predictably higher rate of stability, because they will have had a freedom of choice now generally unavailable. Today those who do not marry and have children by a certain age are penalized: they find themselves alone, excluded, and miserable, on the margins of a society in which everyone else is compartmentalized into lifetime generational families, chauvinism and exclusiveness their chief characteristic. (Only in Manhattan is single living even tolerable, and that can be debated.) Most people are still forced into marriage by family pressure, the "shotgun," economic considerations, and other reasons that have nothing to do with choice of life style. In our new reproductive unit, however, with the limited contract (see below), childrearing so diffused as to be practically eliminated, economic considerations nonexistent, and all participating members having entered only on the basis of personal preference, "unstable" reproductive social structures will have disappeared.

This unit I shall call a *household* rather than an extended family. The distinction is important: The word *family* implies biological reproduction and some degree of division of labor by sex, and thus the traditional dependencies and resulting power relations, extended over generations; though the size of the family—in this case, the larger numbers of the "extended" family—may affect the strength of this hierarchy, it does not change its structural definition. "Household," however, connotes only a large grouping of people living together for an unspecified time, and with no specified set of interpersonal relations. How would a "household" operate?

Limited Contract. If the household replaced marriage perhaps we would at first legalize it in the same way—if this is necessary at all. A group of ten or so consenting adults of varying ages* could apply for a license as a group in much the same way as a young couple today applies for a marriage license, perhaps even undergoing some form of ritual ceremony, and then might proceed in the same way to set up house. The household license would, however, apply only for a given period, perhaps seven to ten years, or whatever was decided on as the minimal

---

* An added advantage of the household is that if allows older people past their fertile years to share fully in parenthood when they so desire.

time in which children needed a stable structure in which to grow up—but probably a much shorter period than we now imagine. If at the end of this period the group decided to stay together, it could always get a renewal. However, no single individual would be contracted to stay after this period, and perhaps some members of the unit might transfer out, or new members come in. Or, the unit could disband altogether.

There are many advantages to short-term households, stable compositional units lasting for only ten-year periods: the end of family chauvinism, built up over generations, of prejudices passed down from one generation to the next, the inclusion of people of all ages in the childrearing process, the integration of many age groups into one social unit, the breadth of personality that comes from exposure to many rather than to (the idiosyncrasies of) a few, and so on.

Children. A regulated percentage of each household—say one-third—would be children. But whether, at first, genetic children created by couples within the household, or at some future time —after a few generations of household living had severed the special connection of adults with "their" children—children were produced artificially, or adopted, would not matter: (minimal) responsibility for the early physical dependence of children would be evenly diffused among all members of the household.

But though it would still be structurally sound, we must be aware that as long as we use natural childbirth methods, the "household" could never be a totally liberating social form. A mother who undergoes a nine-month pregnancy is likely to feel that the product of all that pain and discomfort "belongs" to her ("To think of what I went through to have you!"). But we want to destroy this possessiveness along with its cultural reinforcements so that no one child will be *a priori* favored over another, so that children will be loved for their own sake.

But what if there is an instinct for pregnancy? I doubt it. Once we have sloughed off cultural superstructures, we may uncover a sex instinct, the normal consequences of which *lead* to pregnancy. And perhaps there is also an instinct to care for the young once they arrive. But an instinct for pregnancy itself would be superfluous—could nature anticipate man's mastery of reproduction? And what if, once the false motivations for pregnancy had been shed, women no longer wanted to "have" children at all? Might this not be a disaster, given that artificial reproduction is not yet perfected? But women have no special reproductive *obligation* to the species. If they are no longer willing, then artificial methods will have to be developed hurriedly, or, at the very least, satisfactory compensations—other than destructive ego investments—would have to be supplied to make it worth their while.

Adults and older children would take care of babies for as long as they needed it, but since there would be many adults and older children sharing the responsibility—as in the extended family—no one person would ever be involuntarily stuck with it.

Adult/child relationships would develop just as do the best relationships today: some adults might prefer certain children over others, just as some children might prefer certain adults over others—these might become lifelong attachments in which the individuals concerned mutually agreed to stay together, perhaps to form some kind of nonreproductive unit. Thus all relationships would be based on love alone, uncorrupted by objective dependencies and the resulting class inequalities. Enduring relationships between people of widely divergent ages would become common.

Legal Rights and Transfers.   With the weakening and severance of the blood ties, the power hierarchy of the family would break down. The legal structure—as long as it is still necessary—would reflect this democracy at the roots of our society. Women would be identical under the law with men. Children would no longer be "minors," under the patronage of "parents"—they would have full rights. Remaining physical inequalities could be legally compensated for: for example, if a child were beaten, perhaps he could report it to a special simplified "household" court where he would be granted instant legal redress.

Another special right of children would be the right of immediate transfer: if the child for any reason did not like the household into which he had been born so arbitrarily, he would be helped to transfer out. An adult on the other hand—one who had lived one span in a household (seven to ten years)—might have to present his case to the court, which would then decide, as do divorce courts today, whether he had adequate grounds for breaking his contract. A certain number of transfers within the seven-year period might be necessary for the smooth functioning of the household, and would not be injurious to its stability as a unit so long as a core remained. (In fact, new people now and then might be a refreshing change.) However, the unit, for its own best economy, might have to place a ceiling on the number of transfers in or out, to avoid depletion, excessive growth, and/or friction.

Chores. As for housework: The larger family-sized group (probably about fifteen people) would be more practical—the waste and repetition of the duplicate nuclear family unit would be avoided, e.g., as in shopping or cooking for a small family, without the loss of intimacy of the larger communal experiment. In the interim, any housework would have to be rotated equitably; but eventually cybernation could automate out almost all domestic chores.

City Planning. City planning, architecture, furnishings, all would be altered to reflect the new social structure. The trend toward mass-produced housing would probably continue, but the housing might be designed and even built (perhaps out of prefabricated components) by the people living there to suit their own needs and tastes. Privacy could be built in: either through private rooms in every household, or with "retreats" within the larger city to be shared by people of other households, or both. The whole might form a complex the size of a small town or a large campus. Perhaps campus is the clearer image: We could have small units of self-determined housing—prefabricated component parts set up or dismantled easily and quickly to suit the needs of the limited contract—as well as central permanent buildings to fill the needs of the community as a whole, i.e., perhaps the equivalent of a "student union" for socializing, restaurants, a large computer bank, a modern communications center, a computerized library and film center, "learning centers" devoted to various specialized interests, and whatever else might be necessary in a cybernetic community.

The Economy. The end of the family structure would necessitate simultaneous changes in the larger economy. Not only would reproduction be qualitatively different, so would production: just as we have had to purify relations with children of all external considerations we would first have to have, to be entirely successful in our goals, the socialism of a cybernetic industrial state, aiming not just to redistribute drudgery equitably, but, eventually, to eliminate it altogether. With the further development and wise use of machines, people could be freed from toil, "work" divorced from wages and redefined: Now both adults and children could indulge in serious "play" as much as they wanted.

In the transition, as long as we still had a money economy, people might receive a guaranteed annual income from the state to take care of basic physical needs. These incomes, distributed equitably to men, women, and children, regardless of age, work, prestige, birth, would in themselves equalize in one blow the economic class system. . . .

Thus, in the larger context of a cybernetic socialism, the establishment of the household as the alternative to the family for reproduction of children, combined with every imaginable life style for those who chose to live singly or in nonreproductive units, would resolve all the basic dilemmas that now arise from the family to obstruct human happiness. Let us go over our four minimal demands to see how our imaginary construction would fare.

(1) *The freeing of women from the tyranny of their biology by any means available, and the diffusion of the childbearing and childrearing role to the society as a whole, to men and other children as well as women.* This has been corrected. *Childbearing* could be taken over by technology, and if this proved too much against our past tradition and psychic structure (which it certainly would at first) then adequate incentives and compensations would have to be developed—other than the ego rewards of possessing the child—to reward women for their special social contribution of pregnancy and childbirth. Most of *childrearing*, as we have seen, has to do with the maintaining of power relations, forced internalization of family traditions, and many other ego concerns that war with the happiness of the individual child. This repressive socialization process would now be unnecessary in a society in which the interests of the individual coincided with those of the larger society. Any childrearing responsibility

left would be diffused to include men and other children equally with women. In addition, new methods of instant communication would lessen the child's reliance on even this egalitarian primary unit.

(2) *The economic independence and self-determination of all.* Under socialism, even if still a money economy, work would be divorced from wages, the ownership of the means of production in the hands of all the people, and wealth distributed on the basis of need, independent of the social value of the individual's contribution to society. We would aim to eliminate the dependence of women and children on the labor of men, as well as all other types of labor exploitation. Each person could choose his life style at will, changing it to suit his tastes without seriously inconveniencing anyone else; no one would be bound into any social structure against his will, for each person would be totally self-governing as soon as he was physically able.

(3) *The total integration of women and children into the larger society.* This has been fulfilled: The concept of childhood has been abolished, children having full legal, sexual, and economic rights, their educational/work activities no different from those of adults. During the few years of their infancy we have replaced the psychologically destructive genetic "parenthood" of one or two arbitrary adults with a diffusion of the responsibility for physical welfare over a larger number of people. The child would still form intimate love relationships, but instead of developing close ties with a decreed "mother" and "father," the child might now form those ties with people of his own choosing, of whatever age or sex. Thus all adult-child relationships will have been mutually chosen—equal, intimate relationships free of material dependencies. Correspondingly, though children would be fewer, they would not be monopolized, but would mingle freely throughout the society to the benefit of all, thus satisfying that legitimate desire to be around the young which is often called the reproductive "instinct."

(4) *Sexual freedom, love, etc.* So far we have not said much of love and sexual freedom because there is no reason for it to present a problem: there would be nothing obstructing it. With full license human relationships eventually would be redefined

for the better. If a child does not know his own mother, or at least does not attach a special value to her over others, it is unlikely that he would choose her as his first love object, only to have to develop inhibitions on this love. It is possible that the child might form his first close physical relationships with people his own size out of sheer physical convenience, just as men and women, all else being equal, might prefer each other over those of the same sex for sheer physical fit. But if not, if he should choose to relate sexually to adults, even if he should happen to pick his own genetic mother, there would be no *a priori* reasons for her to reject his sexual advances, because the incest taboo would have lost its function. The "household," a transient social form, would not be subject to the dangers of inbreeding.

Thus, without the incest taboo, adults might return within a few generations to a more natural "polymorphously perverse" sexuality, the concentration on genital sex and orgasmic pleasure giving way to total physical/emotional relationships that *included* that. Relations with children would include as much genital sex as the child was capable of—probably considerably more than we now believe—but because genital sex would no longer be the central focus of the relationship, lack of orgasm would not present a serious problem. Adult/child and homosexual sex taboos would disappear, as well as nonsexual friendship (Freud's aim-inhibited love). All close relationships would include the physical, our concept of exclusive physical partnerships (monogamy) disappearing from our psychic structure, as well as the construct of a Partner Ideal. But how long it would take for these changes to occur, and in what forms they would appear, remains conjecture. The specific need not concern us here. We need only set up the preconditions for a free sexuality: whatever forms it took would be assuredly an improvement on what we have now, "natural" in the truest sense.

In the transitional phase, adult genital sex and the exclusiveness of couples within the household might have to be maintained in order for the unit to be able to function smoothly, with a minimum of internal tension caused by sexual frictions. It is unrealistic to impose theories of what *ought* to be on a psyche already fundamentally organized around specific emotional needs. And this is why individual attempts to eliminate sexual possessiveness are now always inauthentic. We would do much better to concentrate on altering the social structures that have produced this psychical organization, allowing for the eventual—if not in our lifetime—fundamental restructuring (or should I say destructuring?) of our psychosexuality.